W9-ARS-106

You Can't Keep Slope Down

& Other Skill-Building Math Activities

GRADES 8–9

Faye Nisonoff Ruopp & Paula Poundstone

HEINEMANN
Portsmouth, NH

Heinemann
A division of Reed Elsevier Inc.
361 Hanover Street
Portsmouth, NH 03801–3912
www.heinemann.com

Offices and agents throughout the world

Library of Congress Cataloging-in-Publication Data
Ruopp, Faye Nisonoff.
  You can't keep slope down : and other skill-building math activities, grades 8–9 /
Faye Nisonoff Ruopp & Paula Poundstone.
      p. cm. — (The math with a laugh series)
  Includes bibliographical references.
  ISBN-10: 0-325-00928-7
  ISBN-13: 978-0-325-00928-5
  1. Mathematics—Study and teaching (Middle School)—Activity programs.
2. Mathematics—Study and teaching (Secondary)—Activity programs.   I. Poundstone,
Paula.   II. Title.   III. Series: Ruopp, Faye Nisonoff. Math with a Laugh series.
  QA135.6.R8642 2007
  510.71'2—dc22   2006100259

Editor: Leigh Peake
Production: Abigail M. Heim
Typesetter: Gina Poirier Design
Cover and interior design: Joni Doherty Design
Cover and interior illustrations: Michael Kline (www.dogfoose.com)
Manufacturing: Louise Richardson

Printed in the United States of America on acid-free paper
11 10 09 08 07 VP 1 2 3 4 5

To Charlie & Marcus,
for making my life infinitely joyful.

—*Faye*

To Toshia, Alley & Thomas E,
without whom nothing adds up. Thank you.

—*Paula*

Contents

Patterns, Relations & Algebra

Geometry

Measurement

Data Analysis, Statistics & Probability

Preface

When we first decided to collaborate on a mathematics book, we had in mind the creation of problems to be done during the summer. Schools have a long tradition of assigning summer reading; many teachers ask for parallel assignments in mathematics so that students do not lose ground over the summer months. Doing math in the summer—what a thought! Of course, many students will wonder why anyone would create math problems for vacation time. Believe it or not, we're sympathetic to that feeling. And that's why we've created a set of problems that we hope will be different from those found in standard textbooks—different in tone and style, but not in content. These problems are intentionally silly and humorous so students can laugh and be serious about the mathematics, all at the same time!

There has actually been some analysis of the benefits of humor in mathematics classrooms. In the December 2004/January 2005 edition of *Mathematics Teaching in the Middle School*, George and Janette Gadanidis and Alyssa Huang state,

> There are several benefits to using humor in the mathematics classroom (Cornett 1986, 2001; Dyer 1997; Martin and Baksh 1995; Medgyes 2002; Wischnewski 1986):
>
> • Humor helps create a more positive learning environment. It helps reduce barriers to communication and increase rapport between teacher and students.
>
> • Humor helps gain students' attention and keep their interest in a classroom activity.
>
> • By reducing stress and anxiety, humor helps improve comprehension and cognitive retention.
>
> • Humor improves students' attitudes toward the subject.
>
> • Humor helps communicate to students that it is okay for them to be creative; to take chances; to look at things in an offbeat way; and perhaps, even make mistakes in the process.

• Humor can help students see concepts in a new light and increase their understanding.

• The use of humor is rewarding for the teacher, knowing that students are listening with enjoyment. (10 [5]:245)

Although designed for use in the summer, these problems can also serve as a supplement to the curriculum during the academic year, as math to do at home with parents, as well as for skills reinforcement. Students need a change of pace and environment at times. These problems were created to provide entertaining contexts while keeping the mathematics content targeted and sound. The problems can be used as assessments, assignments, additional practice, or extra credit, as well as summer work. In addition, you will note as you scan the problems that there is a good deal of reading involved, making them an excellent tool for students to practice reading in context. We assume, then, that these materials could also be used for reading practice with students.

We ended up with a series of three books, one each for grades 4 and 5, 6 and 7, and 8 and 9. The content for these grade-level books is based on the focus areas identified in state and national standards. These areas, however, may vary from school to school. You may therefore choose to use problems from different grade-level books to accommodate your needs. Our goal was to make the materials as flexible as possible.

Whenever we look at mathematics materials, we tend to be curious about the authors, wanting to know who they are and why they wrote the materials at hand. So we've each included a short piece about ourselves, since we think our story is one that may both surprise and entertain you.

From Faye Nisonoff Ruopp

Paula Poundstone was a student of mine in the 1970s at Lincoln-Sudbury Regional High School in Sudbury, Massachusetts. Paula would say that she was never very good at math; I would say quite the contrary. I saw potential. Paula went on to be a highly successful comedian after she graduated, and we have remained close over the past thirty-two years. Paula now has her own children who are studying mathematics, and at times, I get calls (some of them late at night) about how to do some of the math problems they get in school. Once Paula told me that she made up stories for the problems to make them easier for her children to understand. Given her comedic talents, these stories turned out to be gems. And that's when the idea of collaborating on these books occurred to us. So now, after thirty-two years, she and I can proudly say that she has written a math book with her math teacher, an accomplishment that makes us both smile. We've come full circle, and we think this book is symbolic, in many ways, of the special relationships that students and teachers form, of the humanity that characterizes the study of mathematics, and of the belief that all students can learn and enjoy doing mathematics—and even smile through it all!

Many teachers hope to make mathematics playful and friendly for their students. I would like to extend the opportunity to parents as well. In thinking about my experiences as a parent doing mathematics together with my son, Marcus (who has far surpassed my mathematical abilities, I am proud to admit), I recall fondly the times when we sat down together to tackle a tough problem and the car rides when I posed problems such as "We've decided you can go to bed a half hour later each year. At some point you won't be going to sleep at all. How old will you be then?" He worked on that problem for an hour on our way to Vermont one weekend, not knowing anything about fractions. I also recall when he was about five, I asked him, "What would happen if you subtracted six from two?" His response: "You would get four in minus land!" His connection of mathematics to some fantasy world of negative numbers reminds me how important it is for children to experience their own inventions and perceptions of how mathematics makes sense to them. Likewise, Paula's fantasy contexts, rooted in humor and humanity, enable us to laugh while at the same time thinking hard about how the mathematics works.

From Paula Poundstone

How come math makes people cry? You'd think, of all subjects, history would be the tear jerker. But I cried over math when I was a kid. My mother used to cry when I asked her to help me. My high school math teacher and coauthor of this book, Faye Ruopp, kept a box of tissues on her desk, and if she ran out, class had to be canceled.

I can remember, when I was a kid, I'd get a word problem, something like: "Mary had four apples. She shared two of them with Joe. How many does she have left?"

Although I could calculate the remaining apples, I mostly wanted to know more about Mary and Joe and would often include that curiosity in my homework. Were they just friends? How did Mary get the apples? Why couldn't Joe take care of himself? What is it with Joe? Was that even his real name?

So when my own daughters were so frustrated and intimidated by their elementary school math assignments that they, too, followed the time-honored tradition of shedding buckets of tears over the wonderful world of math, I began to write personalized practice problems for them. Not surprisingly, once the problems seemed less serious, they relaxed a bit and much of the drama slipped away. We have also spent the last few summers doing a page or two of math each day and, no duh, both girls took a huge leap in their math ability as a result. I think the main thing is that it increased their confidence so they hit the ground running in the fall. We've saved lots of money on tissues and I'm hoping you will too.

I think the idea of our writing a book of these kinds of problems came from Ms. Ruopp. She had called me because she was going over her grade book from 1976 and noticed I still had some assignments missing. We got talking and I told her about doing math with my kids and the next thing you know...

And so we offer you these problems in the spirit of improving understanding and increasing rapport with your audience. We hope that when your students do these problems, they will smile and perhaps even laugh, and come to realize that mathematics can be fun and challenging and enlightening, all at once!

Acknowledgments

From Faye

My first memories of mathematics come from my paternal grandfather, Morris Nisonoff, who was a butcher in Jamesburg, New Jersey. He could add a column of numbers faster than anyone I know. I found that fascinating. My gratitude goes to him, then, for making calculations seem fun and accessible. To my own father, I express my love and gratitude for spending time doing math problems with me as a young child many mornings before I went to school. He thought a great way to start the day was to tackle two-digit multiplication! As an accountant, he too had a knack for working with numbers that transferred to both me and my sister, as we each eventually became mathematics teachers. My father, mother, and grandfather taught me the importance of doing mathematics at home with children, and the key role parents play in creating a positive disposition toward math. To that end, doing math with my own son, Marcus, has been a highlight of my parenting. I thank him, especially for continuing a tradition of math study as an applied mathematics major at Yale. His positive and joyful approach to mathematics mirrors his approach to life—how he makes me smile!

I would also like to acknowledge my past and present students, who taught me what it means to come to understand mathematics, and what it means to struggle with a subject that for many is formidable. Their spirit, humanity, diligence, and enthusiasm are continually inspiring. Teaching them has been a gift.

To my friends and family and colleagues in education who encouraged me to write this series, I thank you for your support and faith in this project. You will see yourselves in some of the problems we've created, and we hope they make you laugh.

I would like to thank Ellen Lubell for her impeccable legal expertise and advice in addressing the contractual issues, and for her support as a friend and confidante.

I extend my deepest gratitude to Leigh Peake at Heinemann, who had the vision and courage to support the initial idea for this project. I am indebted to her for her continued influence on the series. A special thanks to Michael Kline for his artistic genius in creating the cartoon illustrations, capturing the essence of the problems and adding to the spirit of the contexts. I also want to thank Abby Heim and Beth Tripp for their care, expertise, and mathematical acuity in editing the series.

Alec Marshall, former chair of the mathematics department at Lincoln-Sudbury Regional High School, hired me for my first teaching position. I continue to be deeply grateful to him for his inspiration as a master teacher and also as an extraordinary human being.

Dr. Peter Braunfeld, Professor Emeritus at the University of Illinois, gave me my first National Science Foundation grant in mathematics professional development when he was a program officer in 1992. I am profoundly grateful to him for making me keenly aware that mathematics as a human endeavor and mathematics as an intellectual pursuit are not mutually exclusive.

And of course, my heartfelt thanks goes to my coauthor, Paula Poundstone, whose comic genius continues to inspire me. Beyond her creativity and sense of humor, she is a remarkable human being and a fabulous mother. Collaborating with Paula on this project has been infinitely rewarding—we laughed so much more than we thought we would! She has proven herself to be the mathematician I always knew she was.

And finally, I want to thank my husband, Charlie, for his unconditional support and calming influence throughout this project. As Paula's high school biology teacher, he also appreciated her amazing talent and encouraged our collaboration. This project never would have happened without him.

From Paula

The fact that I have been a part of the creation of a math book defies the laws of probability. Simple mathematical reasoning tells us that there must have been some other important factors that made this improbability possible.

I'd like to thank Leigh Peake at Heinemann for her kind support and skill. Someday I hope to remove a thorn from her paw.

I thank Abby M. Heim for making my part make sense.

I greatly appreciate the technical support of my assistant, Carmen Cannon, and that of my friend, Gordon McKee.

I will always be in the debt of my manager, Bonnie Burns, for clearing the path for me for thirteen years.

Faye Nisonoff Ruopp has been my friend, teacher, and mentor for thirty-three years. My admiration and appreciation of her grows exponentially each day. Without Faye, who knows what n would equal?

Number Sense & Operations

The problems that follow are in the Number Sense and Operations strand. The mathematics in these problems focuses on ordering real numbers and an understanding of ratio and proportion. Students in grades 8 and 9 also study exponents and their use in scientific notation as well as absolute value and simplification of numerical and algebraic expressions. The topics for these problems were chosen from state and national standards:

- Compare and order integers, rational numbers, decimals, and percents

- Define common irrational numbers, such as the square root of 2 and pi

- Use ratios and proportions in the solution of problems involving unit rates and scale factors

- Represent numbers in scientific notation

- Use the associative, commutative, and distributive properties

- Simplify numerical expressions, including absolute value

Number Sense & Operations

Folding for the Sheer Joy of It

With a crisp snap of your wrist, you shook a blue denim shirt out in front of you, holding it by the shoulder seams, which you quickly matched up and pinched evenly together. The crowd of 30,000 excited onlookers *oohed* and *aahed* with admiration and approval.

You have enjoyed folding all of your life. The sheer joy you feel when you transform an unruly pile of puffy, hot, just-dried laundry into a disciplined stack of flat cloth units can't even be imagined by most people, but never in your wildest dreams had you thought that this pleasurable activity could bring you a chance to win a million dollars. Yet, there you were at the finals of the Worldwide Folding Competition in the host country of Unsk.

Your turn was just after the Unskian competitor, who, not surprisingly, had the enthusiastic support of the hometown crowd. You stepped to a table on the arena floor and began folding a pile of towels with military precision. You folded twenty and stacked them like paper in a heartbeat. At the next table you grabbed some boxer shorts, aligned the legs, and gave a quick karate chop to fold them down the middle. It was poetry.

There were a few more wrinkles in your folding performance at the next three tables as the degree of difficulty increased. You folded a six-man tent into the size of a corncob, but even after two attempts, a flap kept hanging out. You got dizzy folding a circular tablecloth, and the set of hand towels and facecloths that you

Worldwide Folding

You Can't Keep Slope Down by Faye Nisonoff Ruopp and Paula Poundstone (Heinemann: Portsmouth, NH), © 2007.

folded into a decorative clipper ship shape capsized. But you still had a shot at the grand prize or certainly an endorsement deal.

At least it seemed that way until you got to the last table, with the fitted sheet. The fitted sheet is that truly unmanageable piece of cloth with elastic at the corners that goes over the mattress. This one may have been alive.

After twenty minutes you were wrapped so tightly inside it, it took two judges to cut you out.

You quickly checked your scores:

$$120\% \quad -\frac{1}{16} \quad .\overline{6} \quad \sqrt{2} \quad -\frac{5}{9} \quad \frac{9}{8}$$

You were allowed to throw out the lowest score, but which one was it?

Put them in order from least to greatest.

You Can't Keep Slope Down by Faye Nisonoff Ruopp and Paula Poundstone (Heinemann: Portsmouth, NH), © 2007.

Looking for Pi in All the Wrong Places

It happens every year. It's as dependable as the arrival of baby chicks in the spring, static cling in the winter, and acne on picture day. The students who don't study flock to Pete's Pies on the night before the geometry midterm exam to learn about pi. They think pie is pi, but it's not, it's pie. Pi is pi. They're the same kids who got caught on the "What are naval stores?" question on the colonial history test. They nervously wrote, "The place the Navy buys its hats, anchors, beans, and stuff," onto the test paper, the not so bright thinking they were geniuses ("I didn't even need to study!") and the fairly intelligent suspecting a trap.

Devon wasn't the kind of guy to put much wear and tear on the binding of a textbook, so there he sat at the counter, eating pie to learn about pi. Raul cleaned the tables, wiped the counters, mopped the floors, and distributed the tabletop advertisements for next week's pie of the week while watching Devon eat. Devon ate strawberry pie, peach pie, mince pie, blueberry pie, strawberry-peach pie, strawberry-mince pie, strawberry-blueberry pie, mince-peach pie, mince-blueberry pie, chocolate pie, Boston crème pie, Cleveland crème pie, Las Vegas crème pie, and pecan pie. Raul couldn't stand it any longer.

You Can't Keep Slope Down by Faye Nisonoff Ruopp and Paula Poundstone (Heinemann: Portsmouth, NH), © 2007.

"Hey, man, are you trying to learn about pi?" he asked.

"Yeah," Devon answered, his voice muffled through crust. "I've had thirteen pieces of pie and I still don't get it."

"You've had fourteen pieces, but that's not the way to do it."

"Why, is this a salad fork?" asked Devon.

"No, man, it's pi, not pie. It's about the relationship between the parts of a circle."

"Oh," said Devon, spraying crust crumbs.

Raul grabbed a ruler and some string and gave an inspired lesson on pi, using pie plates, counter stools, coffee cups, and a silver dollar. After each demonstration a shout went up from the gathering crowd of students.

"You are so cool, Raul!" shouted a guy in a hooded sweatshirt in the back. "Do you know anything about colonial history? I've got a makeup test next week."

"Sure," said Raul. "Come back; next week is potato-pineapple pie week."

"That's OK—we'll read the textbook," the hooded guy answered back.

Explain the meaning of pi in your own words. Be sure to include how it relates to circles and its approximate value. Don't get any blueberries on the paper.

You Can't Keep Slope Down by Faye Nisonoff Ruopp and Paula Poundstone (Heinemann: Portsmouth, NH), © 2007.

Have I Got a Deal for You

So far Wilamena has mostly enjoyed her stay at the Peak Performance Lacrosse Camp. The coaching is really solid and the more effort she puts in, the more her lacrosse skills improve, and she knows that that's the best deal an athlete in training can get. However, some deals she has made at camp haven't worked out so well. She thought it was a good deal to agree to be the last in her cabin to shower so she wouldn't have to rush while the other girls waited, but the hot water ran out just after she soaped up, and she was forced to spring out from the icy-cold spray. She still had bubbles under her armpits until her forty-third jumping jack during the morning workout.

During the pregame warm-up later that day, another camper missed catching the ball and offered to buy Wilamena an ice cream if she'd go get the ball. So, thinking that was a great deal, Wilamena bounced along behind that hard rubber ball down the side of the Peak Performance Mountain peak, into the lake at the bottom. The snapping turtle that fastened itself to her left toe while she swam after the ball let go about halfway through her hike back up the mountain. She missed the game altogether, which was just as well since she needed the time to scratch the poison ivy rash she had contracted

You Can't Keep Slope Down by Faye Nisonoff Ruopp and Paula Poundstone (Heinemann: Portsmouth, NH), © 2007.

on her way back with the ball. Still, as she sat picking the burrs out of her hair while eating her ice cream, she decided she was going to check her future deals out a little more carefully.

The camp store offers 3 lacrosse balls for $5.49 in package A or 8 balls for $13.76 in package B. Now that she's being more careful, which package should Wilamena buy?

Pass the Waffles, Please, Pocahontas

Last year I called Faye Ruopp and, on behalf of the 4 members of the Poundstone family, invited the 3 members of the Ruopp family to Thanksgiving dinner. She said, "That sounds nice."

I said, "Yeah, we don't eat a turkey dinner, and I've read that there's evidence that the Pilgrims didn't either. We eat waffles shaped like Tweety Bird cooked in a waffle iron that looks like Sylvester the cat, which is what I think the Pilgrims would have eaten if they had had an electrical outlet nearby."

She said, "Oh, um, isn't your table kind of small to fit all of us?"

I said, "That's OK; we sometimes just put a tablecloth on the floor and enjoy kind of an indoor picnic.

"So, the 5 of us eat 7 waffles. Should we assume the same proportion for you?"

She said, "There's only 4 of you."

I said, "Yes, but on Thanksgiving we let the dog eat with us."

She said, "Charlie has to work that day."

I said, "He's a school principal. He works on Thanksgiving?"

You Can't Keep Slope Down by Faye Nisonoff Ruopp and Paula Poundstone (Heinemann: Portsmouth, NH), © 2007.

She said, "There have been a lot of discipline problems next year. They're having detentions on Thanksgiving. I just remembered."

I said, "Oh, well, maybe next year."

If they come next year and they eat the same proportion of waffles as the 5 of us, how many waffles will we need for everyone?

You Can't Keep Slope Down by Faye Nisonoff Ruopp and Paula Poundstone (Heinemann: Portsmouth, NH), © 2007.

Number Sense & Operations

And Let Me Tell You Something Else

I have an unfortunate tendency to lecture my children. It doesn't help when we have a problem; it's just my way. If you have a parent like this, I beg you to have mercy on him or her. Most parents who lecture would sit quietly and let their children learn from their mistakes by themselves if they possibly could.

I stumbled into bed exhausted from lecturing my daughter Toshia the other night. She was supposed to memorize the mass of the moon for a science test and be able to write it in both scientific notation and standard form. She said that it was "stupid" and that she didn't need to know the mass of the moon because she was going to be a famous singer. I then gave her a good, solid ten-minute lecture, made up right there on the spot, on the fact that she doesn't know the future any more than the rest of us and therefore can't possibly have any idea whether the knowledge of the moon's mass, in both scientific notation and standard form, will be important to her or not, but that her very own life experience can already inform her that her present situation can be greatly improved by following directions, acting responsibly, and getting good grades. And that, by the way, some of the best songs ever written, "Moon Shadow," "Moondance," and "Moon River," feature the moon, and anyone singing about the moon might do it just that much more beautifully if she knew its mass and could write it in scientific notation as well as standard form.

You Can't Keep Slope Down by Faye Nisonoff Ruopp and Paula Poundstone (Heinemann: Portsmouth, NH), © 2007.

Then I told her to finish studying and go brush her teeth. She made the mistake of telling me she didn't care about brushing her teeth and I gave her another ten-minute lecture about the importance of oral hygiene, which branched off into various barely related topics such as the work habits of the beaver.

So, it's no wonder I fell into a strange nightmare the minute my troubled head hit the pillow. I dreamed that my children—Toshia, Alley, and Thomas E— and I were rocketing toward our long-awaited opportunity of colonizing the moon. It's something I've wanted for a long time, because I hate billboards. We were careening through space, with our hair blown back, toward the dusty gray moon, when an alarm sounded on the control panel. I looked at the panel's computer screen and in enormous red letters, it said, "TO AVOID CRASH- ING TO A PAINFUL DEATH IN JUST A FEW SECONDS, USE THE KEYPAD TO ENTER THE MOON'S MASS."

I screamed, "Toshia, get over here!" and with all of the courage my fifteen-year-old wonder woman could muster, she charged toward the control panel, but just before she began to type, the words "IN STANDARD FORM ONLY, PLEASE" flashed on the screen. Toshia froze, a look of horror tinged with regret on her face, and she wailed, "I can't convert the scientific notation of moon mass to standard form!"

I said, "That's why I told you to..." and we crashed. I awoke in a sweat and quite upset, not so much because we had crashed as because my lecture had been cut short.

Just to prevent your own crashing, if the mass of the moon is 7.35×10^{22} kilograms, write this mass in standard form.

You Can't Keep Slope Down by Faye Nisonoff Ruopp and Paula Poundstone (Heinemann: Portsmouth, NH), © 2007.

An Interest in Interest

Fourteen-year-old Genevieve hadn't had a need in her lifetime that had not been met at its onset, nor had she ever been left to yearn for anything unnecessary for very long. Her wish had been her parents' command pretty much from the start, except when she wished that it not be. Genevieve came to believe that the earth's axis was a very long roll of silver dollars and that it turned at her request.

On the occasion of her birth, her parents had invested $150.00 in a bank account with an annual interest rate of 6%, and Genevieve had always been told that she could withdraw the money when she was fifteen. Therefore, for years, instead of offering her thoughts, companionship, or personal sacrifice, which are the true currency of friendship, she often tried to bribe people to get what she wanted. "If you'll be my friend," she would say, "I'll give you some of my fortune, which is accumulating at 6% each year." Of course, it didn't work on everyone, but it worked on a lot of people. She was almost always first in line at school; she hardly ever did her own homework (which didn't much matter because she usually got someone to give her the test answers by offering the person yet another share of her soon-to-be-released "fortune"). If she liked another kid's outfit, she generally went home with it. She had star billing in the school production of *The Sound of Music* even though she was only actually in it for a few

You Can't Keep Slope Down by Faye Nisonoff Ruopp and Paula Poundstone (Heinemann: Portsmouth, NH), © 2007.

minutes as an unnamed nun who tattled on Maria.

Genevieve appeared to have it all, and then, about a week before her fifteenth birthday, her math teacher, Ms. Kang, taught her class how to calculate percentages and interest rates.

Genevieve's $150.00 earned 6% interest each year. How much money was in her account after 15 years? Write your answer in exponential form.

Was Genevieve first in line the next day?

You Can't Keep Slope Down by Faye Nisonoff Ruopp and Paula Poundstone (Heinemann: Portsmouth, NH), © 2007.

The Whiney Briney Preschool by the Sea

The Whiney Briney Preschool by the Sea is appropriately named. The school is devoted to four- and five-year-olds, the smell of sea salt fills the classroom, the beach is the backyard, and my how the students can whine. Some days their teacher, Ms. Suomu, goes home with a terrific headache from the sirenlike wails of their petty complaints. Seagulls often gather at the windows just to harmonize with them.

Everything is too much or too little to the students at the Whiney Briney Preschool by the Sea. Nothing is ever right. Nothing is ever fair. The students on either side of any given student always have more of whatever is good and less of whatever is bad.

Of course, learning how to function in society is the main lesson of preschool, really, so it's natural that lining up, sharing, waiting one's turn, and appropriate use of the glue stick are major hurdles for all kids of this age. The students at the Whiney Briney Preschool by the Sea do seem to be especially challenged in this area, though. They don't get to do many activities because just distributing the supplies is often more than they can handle. Ms. Suomu would say, "We're going to do an art project today. Everyone is going to get some paints."

"I want blue," Diego would shout.

"Yes, Diego," Ms. Suomu would say, covering her ears, "you will get a blue. You will get a red. You will get a green and you will get a yellow, as soon as you stop whining long enough for me to distribute them."

"That's not fair," Lizeth would say in a tone that brought three seagulls to the window nearest her.

"Yes, it is fair, Lizeth. You will get a red. You will get a blue. You will get a green. You will get a yellow, too, as soon you stop whining long enough for me to distribute them."

Austin would jump to her feet. "How come I don't have any paints?" she'd whine.

"Austin, no one has paints yet. Look around," Ms. Suomu would say. "You will get a blue. You will get a red. You will get a green. You will get a yellow, too, as soon as you stop whining long enough for me to distribute them."

There are twenty students. It is always a slow process. (The kids had to start making their valentines on the first day of school.)

Use the distributive property to expand each of these expressions. Think of the terms inside the parentheses as the Whiney Briney Preschool by the Sea students, and make sure each one gets multiplied by the outside factor before the seagulls begin to circle:

A. $4(5x - 3)$

B. $-2(3r + 7)$

Number Sense & Operations

Simple Is Good

Conrad H. Shoshtakoshtavish wished more than anything in the entire world that he wasn't standing in front of the zoo director's desk about to report to her that he had been responsible for today's disaster at the Great Greater Greaterville Zoo, but he was and the director had her hackles up.

"How does one zookeeper manage to lose practically every animal in the zoo, Mr. Um...Mr. Shoshta..."

"Shoshtakoshtavish," said Conrad. "Try pretending to eat a lemon when you say it. It's easier when you're puckered."

"Mr. Shoshtakoshtavish, what happened to the animals?" the director asked, trying to keep her composure.

"Yes, ma'am, well you see, I was standing in the camels' enclosure, trying to feed them according to procedure, when one of the camels came up and said, 'Look at that pigeon over there,' and when I turned, he grabbed my keys and tore around the zoo, unlocking all of the other enclosures," Conrad said.

"Let me get this straight," the director spoke slowly, "you turned away from a talking camel to look at a pigeon?"

"Well, yes, they can be quite interesting," said Conrad, "but as soon as I saw the camel opening those cages, I ignored the pigeon."

 You Can't Keep Slope Down by Faye Nisonoff Ruopp and Paula Poundstone (Heinemann: Portsmouth, NH), © 2007.

"Great," said the director, burying her head in her hands. "Mr. Shostakosh—Mr. Shoshtook—" the director sputtered.

"Lemon," Conrad interjected quickly.

"Mr. Shoshtakoshtavish! What happened to the animals?"

"Oh, yes, well, three hippos headed for the snack shop. Boy, they don't need the calories, huh? They've pretty much already been supersized. And let's see, I caught five zebras just checking themselves out in the mirror in the men's room. Then I saw one hippo go back into his enclosure. A porcupine slipped out and bought a balloon. That's not going to last, huh? Two lions made it all of the way to the Hello Kitty store in the mall. Then two more zebras went into the men's room. I never realized how vain zebras are."

"Mr. Shoshtakoshtavish, could you just simplify the story and quickly tell me how many of each species is accounted for, so we can find and return them all safely before they make unauthorized purchases on the Internet?" the director pleaded.

Simple is good. Can you please simplify the following expression:

$$6 - 3(2 - 7) + |\text{-}3| - 2^3$$

You Can't Keep Slope Down by Faye Nisonoff Ruopp and Paula Poundstone (Heinemann: Portsmouth, NH), © 2007.

Skip Your Homework and Do Schoolwork at Home Instead

The concept of equivalent expressions is not only important in mathematics but also makes for smooth sailing in family life. When my daughter Toshia told me she doesn't like to practice the piano, I said, "Don't practice. Just play. In fact, play every day for about thirty minutes, and play this music that the teacher gave you," and she was happy to do so.

My daughter Alley told me she didn't want to eat dinner the other night. So I said, "Don't eat dinner. I hate dinner. Here, have this salad snack. Oh, and have it at the table with this glass of milk and this pasta treat on a dish. Don't eat dinner, though. I agree, dinner is the worst."

My son, Thomas E, told me one night that he didn't want to go to sleep. So, again I used an equivalent expression. I said, "Then don't go to sleep. You're right, sleep is horrible. I don't know what I was thinking when I said it. I tell you what, instead of sleeping, lie down in your bed, close your eyes, breathe slowly, dream, and drool a little bit. Sleeping is the worst, though, huh?" And he slept like a very tall baby.

You Can't Keep Slope Down by Faye Nisonoff Ruopp and Paula Poundstone (Heinemann: Portsmouth, NH), © 2007.

Which of the following expressions is equivalent to the expression

$$x(3x + 2) - 6 + 3x - 3 + 5x^2 + 8$$

(just in case my kids say they don't like it ...)?

A. $8x^2 + 3x + 1$

B. $5x^2 + 6x + 1$

C. $13x^2 - 1$

D. $8x^2 + 5x - 1$

You Can't Keep Slope Down by Faye Nisonoff Ruopp and Paula Poundstone (Heinemann: Portsmouth, NH), © 2007.

Extra! Extra!

Do you have a sense that you need more practice on number sense and operations? Try these.

---

1. Order the following set of numbers from least to greatest, without using a calculator:

$$100\% \quad 0 \quad -\frac{1}{9} \quad .\overline{3} \quad \pi \quad -\frac{2}{13} \quad \frac{12}{7}$$

---

2. What does it mean to take the square root of a number?

Explain in your own words, and include how it relates to a square.

---

3. The scale on a map is $\frac{1}{4}$ inch = 1 mile. If the distance on a map from Boston to New Haven is $31\frac{1}{4}$ inches, what is the actual distance between the two cities?

You Can't Keep Slope Down by Faye Nisonoff Ruopp and Paula Poundstone (Heinemann: Portsmouth, NH), © 2007.

4. If Louie can shovel 4 driveways in 3 hours, how many driveways can he shovel in 8 hours?

5. Write the number 3.45×10^{12} in standard form.

6. Write the number 678,000,000,000,000 in scientific notation.

7. **Use the distributive property to expand each expression:**

   A. $-3(5r - 7)$

   B. $6s(s + 7)$

8. **Simplify the following expressions:**

   A. $-7 + 4(3 - 6) + |-5| - 3^2$

   B. $3p(2p - 7) - 5 + 9p + 4p^2 + 1$

You Can't Keep Slope Down by Faye Nisonoff Ruopp and Paula Poundstone (Heinemann: Portsmouth, NH), © 2007.

Teacher Notes

1. Folding for the Sheer Joy of It

Problem 1 asks students to order a set of numbers from least to greatest. Encourage students to use number sense to do a preliminary ordering: a first sorting might involve grouping the negative numbers together as the least numbers and then grouping the positive numbers.

Students should recognize that $-\frac{5}{9}$ is less than $-\frac{1}{16}$. Next, it might be helpful to group the numbers greater than 1 and those less than 1. The numbers 120%, $\sqrt{2}$, and $\frac{9}{8}$ are all greater than 1, and $.\overline{6}$ is less than 1. Therefore a preliminary ordering of the first three numbers would be

$$-\frac{5}{9} \qquad -\frac{1}{16} \qquad .\overline{6}$$

After that, it is often helpful to put the numbers in the same form. If all of the numbers are in decimal form, for example, the comparison is much easier. An approximation of $\sqrt{2}$ is 1.414; students should have a good sense of what $\sqrt{2}$ is as a decimal. (One way to think about $\sqrt{2}$ is to consider that $\sqrt{2}$ is between $\sqrt{1}$ and $\sqrt{4}$, and closer to $\sqrt{1}$. Since $\sqrt{1}$ is 1 and $\sqrt{4}$ is 2, $\sqrt{2}$ has to be between 1 and 2, and closer to 1. Students can then square some decimal numbers between 1 and 1.5 to see how close they can get to 2.) Since 120% is 1.2, and $\frac{9}{8}$ is 1.125, the list of numbers ordered from least to greatest is

$$-\frac{5}{9}, \quad -\frac{1}{16}, \quad .\overline{6}, \quad \frac{9}{8}, \quad 120\%, \quad \sqrt{2}$$

Therefore, the folder could throw out the score of $-\frac{5}{9}$.

In general, decimals are much easier to compare than fractions. It is important for students to move easily from one form of a real number to another. As an extension problem, ask students where they would place $\sqrt{3}$ on the list.

2. Looking for Pi in All the Wrong Places

Problem 2 asks students to define pi. Given any circle, the circumference divided by the diameter is always the same value, pi. The value of pi is a little more than three; a decimal approximation is 3.14, and the fraction often used to approximate its value is $\frac{22}{7}$. In fact, pi is an irrational number, a decimal number that never ends or repeats. The Greek letter π is used to represent pi, although the Greeks themselves never used π to stand for this number. Leonhard Euler (1707–83) was the first to use the Greek letter π. Students will revisit pi throughout their studies in mathematics, as it has applications in surprisingly many areas (geometry, trigonometry, calculus). As an extension, ask students to name at least two more irrational numbers.

3. Have I Got a Deal for You

Problem 3 asks students to compare two different rates: 3 balls for $5.49 and 8 balls for $13.76.

One method that is helpful is to find the unit rate for each ratio: the cost of 1 ball for each package.

For package A, the unit rate would be $5.49 ÷ 3, or $1.83 per ball.

For package B, the unit rate would be $13.76 ÷ 8, or $1.72.

Therefore, package B is the better deal. Students can use calculators to perform these division problems. However, if they are still uncomfortable with decimal division, these problems can provide practice with computation.

Another way to approach this problem is to think about how much a common unit of balls would cost in each package. Since one package is for 3 balls and the other is for 8 balls, students can find what the cost of 24 balls would be for each package (24 is the least common multiple of 8 and 3). For package A, we would need to have 8 packages of 3, or 8 × $5.49, or $43.92. For package B, we would need to have 3 packages of 8, or 3 × $13.76, or $41.28. Therefore, package B is better. Note that finding a unit rate, where the common unit is 1, is simply a special case of finding a common unit. Students will use the ideas of ratio and proportion in all of mathematics and its applications. One of the most important applications is in geometry and trigonometry, as proportions are used to calculate distances and lengths that cannot be measured.

As an extension, ask students to come up with another package that is a better deal than package A but not as good as package B.

4. Pass the Waffles, Please, Pocahontas

Problem 4 asks students to solve a problem that requires setting up a proportion, an equation stating that two ratios are equal. Since 7 waffles feed 5 people, we need to find how many waffles will feed 8 people (the 4 Poundstones and their dog in addition to the 3 Ruopps). The proportion is

$$\frac{7}{5} = \frac{x}{8}.$$

Encourage students to estimate an answer before they solve the proportion. Should the number of waffles be greater than or less than 7? To solve this proportion, multiply both sides of the equation by 8.

$$8\left(\frac{7}{5}\right) = \left(\frac{x}{8}\right)8$$
$$x = \frac{56}{5}, \text{ or } 11.2$$

However, we need to interpret this answer in the context of the problem. It would be difficult to make two-tenths (.2) of a waffle; therefore, rounding up, the Poundstones would be wise to make 12 waffles. As an extension, ask students to find the number of people the Poundstones could invite if they made 50 waffles.

5. And Let Me Tell You Something Else

To solve problem 5, students need to convert a number written in scientific notation (the product of a number greater than or equal to 1 but less than 10 and a power of 10) to standard form (a number written with all of its digits displayed). In this problem, since 10 is being raised to the 22nd power, the decimal point is moved 22 places to the right, and therefore the answer is 73,500,000,000,000,000,000,000.

Students should appreciate that scientific notation is a convenient way of expressing very large (and very small) numbers so that we don't have to write a lot of zeros. Scientific notation also makes comparing large numbers easier, since the powers of 10 in each number tell us immediately about relative sizes, whereas with numbers in standard form, we would have to count all the zeros in the numbers to determine their relative size. As an extension, ask students if they would rather write a google in scientific notation or in standard form! (A google is 10 to the 100th power!)

6. An Interest in Interest

Problem 6 asks students to think about the effect of getting 6% interest per year after 15 years on an initial investment of $150. If students are having difficulty thinking about multiple years, have them write down the calculations they would make for the amount of money they would have at the end of the first year. This amount can be found by first finding 6% of $150 and then adding that amount to $150:

$$(.06)(150) + 150$$

Note that there is a shortcut for performing these operations. If we factor out 150 from each quantity in the sum, we have

$$150(.06 + 1), \text{ or } 150(1.06)$$

Therefore, to find out how much money is in the account after 1 year, we can simply multiply 150 by 1.06. It is helpful for students to think of 1.06 as the result of adding $1 + .06$: the 1 refers to the entire initial amount of $150, and the .06 refers to the 6% of that quantity for interest.

Extending this thinking to the next year (the amount of money in the account after 2 years), we would take 6% of $150(1.06)$ and then add that interest to $150(1.06)$:

$$(.06)[150(1.06)] + 150(1.06)$$

We will not perform these calculations yet because it's useful to see if there is some pattern to the numbers we're getting.

Looking at this sum, $[(.06)[150(1.06)] + 150(1.06)]$, again we can factor out a common factor, which in this case is $150(1.06)$. In doing so, the sum becomes

$$150(1.06)(.06 + 1), \text{ or } 150(1.06)(1.06), \text{ or } 150(1.06)^2$$

This is the amount of money in the account after 2 years. Students at this point should see a pattern: to find the amount in the account after n years, multiply 150 by $(1.06)^n$. Therefore, in 15 years, the amount will be $150(1.06)^{15}$. As an extension, ask students to find how many years it would take for the investment of $150 to triple.

7. The Whiney Briney Preschool by the Sea

To solve problem 7, students need to apply the distributive property of multiplication over subtraction for part A and the distributive property of multiplication over addition for part B. In general, the distributive property is

$$a(b - c) = ab - ac, \text{ and } a(b + c) = ab + ac$$

One way to think about the distributive property is to look at specific numbers. For example, $2(3 + 5)$ could be interpreted as 2 groups of $(3 + 5)$, or 2 groups of 8, or 16. This expression could also be interpreted as 2 groups of 3 added to 2 groups of 5, or $6 + 10$, or 16.

To find the answer for part A, first multiply $4(5x)$, which is $20x$, and then multiply $4(3)$, which is 12. The answer is $20x - 12$. If students do not understand why the answer involves subtraction, they may want to rewrite the original problem as $4(5x + {}^-3)$, since subtracting a number is equivalent to adding its opposite. Now they can use the distributive property as defined for multiplication over addition:

$$4(5x) + 4({}^-3), \text{ or } 20x + {}^-12, \text{ or } 20x - 12$$

For part B, ${}^-2(3r + 7)$, distribute the ${}^-2$:

$${}^-2(3r) + {}^-2(7), \text{ or } {}^-6r - 14$$

Students tend to make many errors when applying the distributive property, the most common of which is to forget to distribute over the second quantity in parentheses. For example, they mistakenly write $3(x + 5) = 3x + 5$. As an extension, ask students to reverse the process—rewrite the following using parentheses: ${}^-15x - 27$.

8. Simple Is Good

For problem 8, students need to use the order of operations, the definition of absolute value, and the distributive property to simplify the expression given. The mnemonic "Please Excuse My Dear Aunt Sally" (PEMDAS) is a common one for students to use to remember the order of operations. In this problem, however, absolute value is present, and PEMDAS does not include absolute value.

Some teachers use GEMDAS as a substitute (G is for grouping); grouping comes first in any simplification, including parentheses and absolute value.

- In this problem, if we begin with computing $|-3|$, the answer is 3.

- The next step is to compute $2 - 7$, the expression in parentheses, which is $^-5$.

- The original expression now becomes $6 - 3(^-5) + 3 - 2^3$.

- Since computing exponents is next in the order of operations, we first find 2^3, or 8. The expression is now $6 - 3(^-5) + 3 - 8$.

- Multiplication is next: $3(^-5)$ is $^-15$, so we have $6 - ^-15 + 3 - 8$.

- Since all of the operations are now addition and subtraction, we perform them left to right: $6 - ^-15$ is $6 + 15$, which is 21; $21 + 3$ is 24; and $24 - 8$ is 16.

As an extension, ask students to make up their own expression that involves exponents, absolute value, and the distributive property, so that the answer is 34, using just the numbers 2, 3, and 4.

9. Skip Your Homework and Do Schoolwork at Home Instead

To solve problem 9, students need to know how to combine like terms (terms with the same variable raised to the same exponent) in algebraic expressions.

- First, students need to use the distributive property to expand $x(3x + 2)$, or $3x^2 + 2x$. The expression now becomes

$$3x^2 + 2x - 6 + 3x - 3 + 5x^2 + 8.$$

- Grouping like terms together, the transformed expression is $(5x^2 + 3x^2) + (3x + 2x) + (8 - 6 - 3)$, or $8x^2 + 5x - 1$.

- The answer, then, is D.

Combining like terms is related to the distributive property, in that we can rewrite $5x^2 + 3x^2$ as $x^2(5 + 3)$, taking out the common factor of x^2. The process of taking out a common factor is known as factoring an expression. As an extension, ask students to factor $9s^3 + 12s^2 - 3s$.

Extra! Extra!

1. $\frac{^-2}{13}$ $\frac{^-1}{9}$ 0 $.\overline{3}$ 100% $\frac{12}{7}$ π

2. The square root of a number is the number that you need to square to get back to the original number. If you consider a square's area as the original number, then the square root of that number is the length of a side of the square.

3. 125 miles

4. $10\frac{2}{3}$

5. 3,450,000,000,000

6. 6.78×10^{14}

7. A. $^-15r + 21$
   B. $6s^2 + 42s$

8. A. $^-23$
   B. $10p^2 - 12p - 4$

$\mathcal{P}$atterns, Relations & Algebra

$\mathcal{T}$he problems that follow are in the Patterns, Relations, and Algebra strand. The mathematics in these problems focuses on developing eighth and ninth graders' ability to identify linear, quadratic, and exponential relationships from tables, graphs, algebraic equations, and situations in words. In addition, students examine the relationships among various representations of a line, determining a line's slope from its graph and from its equation. Students also begin to solve quadratic equations as well as perform operations on polynomial expressions. The topics covered in these problems were chosen from state and national standards:

- Represent and analyze a variety of patterns (linear, quadratic, and exponential) with tables, graphs, words, and symbolic expressions

- Identify the slope of a line and compare linear growth patterns

- Identify the meaning of the variables and constants in $y = mx + b$

- Add, subtract, and multiply polynomials

- Find solutions to quadratic equations

1

Problem

Do Math, Get Gas

President Raymond will long be remembered for his "two birds with one stone" approach to the nation's problems. The U.S. Mint might put out a three-dollar bill just so President Raymond's face can go on the front of it.

His successes will be legendary, just as surely as historians will kick sand over his failures. His plan to improve the country's math skills while curbing our dependency on oil got off to a bit of a rocky start, however. Each citizen was sent a paper bearing a representation of the relationship between two variables, x and y. Those holding a paper with a quadratic relationship between x and y could purchase gasoline on Mondays and Thursdays; those whose paper showed a linear relationship between x and y could purchase gas on Tuesdays and Fridays; and those with a representation of an exponential relationship between x and y could make their gasoline purchases on Wednesdays and Saturdays.

Instead of fewer people coming to the gas station on the first day of the new rule, everyone came. Most people had no idea what kind of relationship between x and y they held on their paper; they came hoping the gas station attendant could tell them. The lines were backed up from sea to shining sea. Workers missed work while waiting in the huge gas-pump lines. Children missed school, which was just as well, since only a handful of math teachers had been able to identify what kind of relationship was on their paper and either get through

You Can't Keep Slope Down by Faye Nisonoff Ruopp and Paula Poundstone (Heinemann: Portsmouth, NH), © 2007.

the line or await their proper purchasing day. The convenience stores at the gas stations bulged with people, who soon bulged with the contents of the convenience store. Every store in the country sold out of those mini doughnuts with the white powdered sugar. The entire nation's weight increased.

Thank goodness there were some math students out there who stepped in to help. Aaron jumped out of his mother's car at a gas station in Phoenix, Arizona, and offered to take a look at other people's papers to help them understand what kind of x-and-y relationship they held, which was incredibly kind since it felt like it was at least a million degrees there, standing on the cement amidst the gas fumes in the Arizona sun. Some of the waiting customers popped popcorn on their car roof.

A. Aaron found a lady sobbing over her paper. "I just broke up with my boyfriend. I'm not good with relationships. I'm never going to get gas," she cried.

"Well, what kind of relationship do you think your x and y have?" asked Aaron, reaching for her paper.

"I think they're just good friends," she sniffed.

"I think you have to plot them first," Aaron said.

"I wish I had plotted my boyfriend," she said, wiping her eyes.

The sobbing lady's paper looked like this:

INPUT, X	OUTPUT, Y
1	5
2	8
3	11
4	14
5	17
6	20

What kind of relationship did x and y have?

B. There's good public transportation in Chicago, so the gas lines were shorter there than in some cities, but still Buster's Gas and Go had cars lined up a mile or so into Lake Michigan. Buster hadn't sold a drop of gas all day because his customers couldn't figure out if they belonged in the linear, quadratic, or exponential group, but he had sold every last one of those putrid Christmas tree– and strawberry-shaped car air fresheners and a wave of nausea had run through the car passengers as a result.

Sixteen-year-old Lois was on her way to school when she saw both the situation and her duty as a responsible math student. She took a look at the paper held by a driver with a van full of children with lips the color of orange traffic safety cones from chip residue, who were also turning green from air fresheners.

This driver had this funny looking thing on his page:

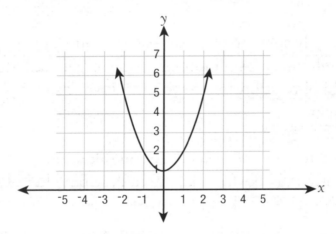

What kind of relationship does it represent between the variables *x* and *y*?

You Can't Keep Slope Down by Faye Nisonoff Ruopp and Paula Poundstone (Heinemann: Portsmouth, NH), © 2007.

C. The line finally started to move, thanks to Lois. The people with quadratic relationships gassed up and the others drove away and waited for their day, which was certainly good news for the cars finally able to pull out of Lake Michigan. Lois was still helping when the first car out of the lake pulled up.

The driver's paper was dripping wet, but Lois could see this table:

INPUT, X	OUTPUT, Y
0	1
1	2
2	4
3	8
4	16
5	32

What kind of relationship does it represent between the variables x and y?

D. Art Finkel didn't care if he got his tank filled or not. He had purchased a sturdy whisk broom while he waited at Fred's Fuel and Food, just outside of Lansing, Michigan. He was earning $20.00 per car sweeping out the cars of his fellow line waiters. He had also bought out all of the baby wipes in the store at $3.25 per container and was selling them for fifty bucks a wipe to desperate mothers with stinky babies, whom he could easily identify by the toxic vapors swirling from their cars. He wanted the lines to be long.

"Let me see your paper," he said to a bewildered older woman who had been sitting at the front of the line since she was much younger.

She showed him this:

Mary ran a race at a steady rate of 3 meters per second. Her distance, y, is the number of meters she ran after x seconds. What kind of relationship is represented by x and y?

"It's a business relationship," he said and shoved the paper back in her hands, leaving her even more baffled.

Can you figure it out?

You Can't Keep Slope Down by Faye Nisonoff Ruopp and Paula Poundstone (Heinemann: Portsmouth, NH), © 2007.

E. "It's Monday and the x and y relationship on my paper is expolindratic, which means that I get to fill my tank whenever I want!" shouted Mr. Gribith, leaning on his horn while edging forward to cut in line, alone inside his vehicle, which was big enough to carry an entire NBA team without anyone having to sit in the way back.

Renatta slowly pedaled her bike up to Mr. Gribith's car.

"What are you doing?" she asked. "There is no such thing as an expolindratic relationship. What does that mean?"

"It means I want a lot of gas because I've got places to go," answered Mr. Gribith, lifting his nose toward the sky.

"In this country we use more gas than humans anywhere else on earth and we're certainly not more human," said Renatta, and she pedaled away to someplace.

Mr. Gribith's paper read

$$y = x^2 + 3$$

which is definitely not an expolindratic relationship. What type is it?

You Can't Keep Slope Down by Faye Nisonoff Ruopp and Paula Poundstone (Heinemann: Portsmouth, NH), © 2007.

You Can't Keep Slope Down

Slope was fifteen years old in 1863. He had been raised in Cambridge, Massachusetts, by his loving parents, who were professors at Harvard University but were tragically killed the year before when a shelf full of calculus textbooks collapsed on them. It might not have been fatal had the textbooks not been the teacher's editions, which are extra heavy. Lying beneath the stack of books, Slope's father used his last bit of strength to reach for the writing materials that he carried in his shirt pocket, which often caused him to drip ink as he walked. He dipped his quill into his inkwell and ruefully wished someone had invented the ballpoint pen during his lifetime. Inside the cover of a calculus textbook that had struck him in the temple only moments before, he weakly penned,

> *Slope, go live out west with Aunt Bessie and Uncle Cliff. Make your life greater than the sum of its parts by adding to the lives of others. Choose happiness. We love you. Be a good math student.*
>
> *Your Loving Father*
>
> *PS: Don't write in textbooks. This was a rare exception.*

Slope, who was named after part of a linear equation, had made it his business to follow his father's final instructions as best as he could. He was warmly welcomed into his aunt and uncle's home. He learned to milk cows and helped out by milking the cow at the aging Widow

Friccus' place each morning, and he studied math in his every free moment. His specialty became—you guessed it— finding slope. Slope became the fastest slope finder in the West, or certainly within a large area.

$\mathcal{A}$. He could find the slope of the line $y = {}^{-}3x + 7$ in a flash. Can you?

$\mathcal{B}$. Slope attended the local one-room schoolhouse out West. Orientation day was very short. Some kids thought he was a bit weird. He didn't know how to rope a calf, he thought guns were dangerous, and he dripped ink everywhere he went.

One day, right in the middle of their Modern Art Studies class while they were studying Whistler, an outlaw kicked the schoolroom door in and strode into the room.

"I'm a fixin' to steal your schoolmarm's money!" he roared, waving his gun about.

"You're joking," said Ms. Bonn, the teacher. "Teachers don't get paid well at all, especially when you consider the value of their contribution to society. You couldn't even buy a bullet with what's in my purse."

"Oh, really?" said the outlaw, looking dumbstruck. Then, rallying, he said, "Then I'll take you."

He made a quick grab for Ms. Bonn, but not before Slope could leap between the two of them, shouting, "Not so fast! I challenge you to find the slope of this figure here," holding up a line graph that luckily he'd just plotted, "and if you can't find it before I do, you'll get out and leave us alone, Outlaw."

"Why you lily-livered…you sidewindin'…you ol'…what did you say?" the outlaw sputtered, eyeing Slope dangerously through narrowed eyes, but apparently forgetting all about his gun.

"Find the slope of this figure faster than me or get out," repeated Slope.

Meanwhile, Antoine, who was a good math student himself, but a bit more practical, snuck out the back and ran for the sheriff. Slope purposely took his time finding the slope, so the outlaw was still clucking and puffing with frustration, turning the figure upside down and sideways, trying to figure its slope, when the sheriff arrived to haul him away. Slope was a hero.

What was the slope of this figure?

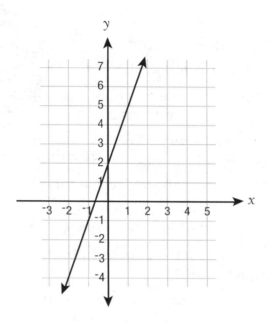

Patterns, Relations & Algebra

Graphing to Blow Their Tops Off

Higgins was a straightlaced fellow, just out of accounting school and new to his job at the Top of the Line Container Tops Company. It was a family-owned business founded generations ago by the great entrepreneur Mr. R. J. Top. Not being a member of the Top family, Higgins was unique to the company, but Uncle Bob, their accountant of sixty-some years (Bob wasn't sure exactly how many; he was fond of rounding off), had tragically died a month or so ago (Bob wasn't exactly sure when) from a paper cut that had developed complications, and the next generation of Top accountants was led by Tiffany, and she was still in middle school and wasn't really applying herself. So they hired Higgins.

Within his first month of going over the books of the Top of the Line Container Tops Company, Higgins had discovered that Uncle Bob had perhaps been a bit too fond of rounding off. The company's financial situation was disastrous. Higgins now stood at the head of a long table in the unenviable position of delivering the bad news to the executives, Uncle Howard, Uncle Buddy, Aunt Doris Mae, and Junior (who couldn't have been a day under ninety). He took a deep breath and heaved a stack of papers onto the end of the long table, pulled a dry-erase marker from his

You Can't Keep Slope Down by Faye Nisonoff Ruopp and Paula Poundstone (Heinemann: Portsmouth, NH), © 2007.

pocket, and turned to the dry-erase board, where he wrote

$$y = {}^-2x + 3$$

"Gentlemen and Lady, everything in these papers can be boiled down to this one equation," he began, and to Higgins' surprise this precipitated a round of congratulatory handshakes, backslapping, and "Way to go's!" from the executives.

"You don't seem to understand," said Higgins. "What this means is, no matter how much this company earns each month, it loses twice as much, although we do receive the $3.00 each month from the trust fund that R. J. Top himself left the company generations ago on the condition that it continue to make only container tops."

Again the executives cheered and celebrated what they clearly viewed as their success.

"I don't think I'm getting through to you!" shouted Higgins over the tops of their gleeful cheers of "We're Tops!"

"The only good news here is that bankruptcy court isn't far away from here and has snack machines that they keep well stocked," Higgins continued. "I think it's time you considered making containers as well as tops. People don't buy just tops."

The room went deadly silent. The steely glares of the executives practically pinned young Higgins to the dry-erase board, until Aunt Doris Mae leaped across the corner of the table toward his throat, shouting, "And give up $3.00 a month? Are you crazy? Are you trying to ruin the Top of the Line Container Tops Company?"

Higgins quickly jumped aside and, in what would have to be called a bizarre coincidence, your class happened to be on a field trip to the Top of the Line Container Tops Company that very day, and you just so happened to be walking by the boardroom window just in time to witness Aunt Doris Mae's head accidentally plow through the tower of paper and Junior grab her by her business-feminine scarf, as Uncle Buddy and Uncle Howard stood by looking as though they were about to beat the hard drive out of poor Higgins as well.

The rest of your class hurried off to the gift shop, but you've never been the type to turn away from someone in trouble, especially when your math skills are in need. You spotted the equation $y = {}^-2x + 3$ on the dry-erase board and, putting concerns for your own safety aside, you ran in and quickly graphed it.

You Can't Keep Slope Down by Faye Nisonoff Ruopp and Paula Poundstone (Heinemann: Portsmouth, NH), © 2007.

$\mathcal{A}$. I know you're not one to brag, but go ahead, graph

$$y = {}^-2x + 3$$

again just to show how you did it.

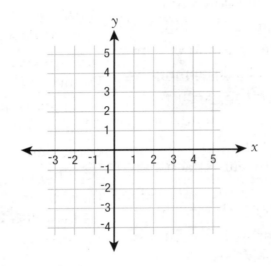

$\mathcal{B}$. Well, fortunately, the executives at Top of the Line Container Tops Company are visual learners. Your courageous graphing really reached them. Now, please write the meaning of the constants $^-2$ and 3 as they relate to the graph. It could mean the difference between life and death for Higgins someday.

24

Like Terms Are No Joke

Mr. Jolly, of Mr. Jolly's Joke Shop, was not happy. April Fool's Day was around the corner and his plastic doggie doo shelf was empty. He had just gotten in a shipment of 1,000 wind-up clacking teeth, which would take years to sell, because wind-up clacking teeth, although classic, are just not that funny. Meanwhile he had received only two exploding diapers, which go like hotcakes. His inventory had gone haywire.

"Kashanda!" he bellowed to his assistant, who was in the back looking for the disappearing ink.

"Yes, Mr. Jolly," she answered, rushing in and coming to a dead stop 5 ft. 6 in. from her boss. She never spoke to him within the range of the squirting flower he wore on his lapel and she certainly never shook his hand.

"Did you count what we have sold and order new products, like I asked you to?" asked Mr. Jolly.

"Yes, sir," Kashanda replied. "And did you put the plastic ice cube with the spider in it in my diet soda?"

"Of course," said Mr. Jolly. "Now, could you tell me how you did the inventory?"

"Sure, I counted how many items we sold and ordered that many more, just like you said, sir," Kashanda said proudly. "And was it you who painted my sunglass lenses black?"

"Why, yes, I did, my dear, but I must ask you, did you not do a separate calculation for each type of item?" Mr. Jolly asked, looking as red as though he had been tricked by the onion-flavored gum and flopping onto his chair, whose whoopie cushion fired off a loud "Barroom!"

"No, sir," Kashanda replied timidly.

"You have to keep like terms together! You cannot add plastic buttocks sales to the sales of the briefcases with the underwear hanging out of them or we'll end up with way too many plastic buttocks, and that wouldn't be funny at all, would it?" Mr. Jolly boomed.

"Yes, sir. I mean, no sir. I see what you're saying, sir. It's like collecting like terms in algebra. By the way, sir, was it you who installed the talking toilet paper holder in my bathroom?"

"Of course it was, my dear, and, look out, you're about to step in plastic vomit."

Remember to collect like terms as you . . .

A. Add the following polynomials:

$$(x^2 + 3x - 7) + (^-2x^2 + 5x - 3)$$

B. Subtract the following polynomials:

$$(6n^2 + 4n - 7) - (2n^2 - 5n + 1)$$

C. Multiply the following binomials:

$$(3r - 5)(^-2r + 1)$$

Bow to Your Partner and Squish 'Im Flat

Farhad was fascinated by the Afro-Brazilian martial art form of capoeira. He had attended a free trial class and enjoyed it very much. Capoeira was invented by African slaves in Brazil in the 1600s. It was a defense art that they made look like a dance so that their captors would not suspect anything. Many capoeira moves use just the legs because a slave's hands were often tied together.

Unfortunately, the fall session of capoeira classes at the activity center was already full when he went to sign up. There was, however, available space in a class in the lesser-known art of swing-pin, a competitive sport that combined Greco-Roman wrestling and square dancing that was developed when things got out of hand at a county fair in the United States in the 1980s. Farhad couldn't sign up for such a compelling sport fast enough.

From that time on, Monday, Wednesday, and Friday afternoons found Farhad at the activity center, struggling happily to master the basics of swing-pin under the skilled and watchful eye of his teacher, "Pummeling" Pete Porter.

"The beauty of this art form," Pummeling Pete used to say, "is that there's always two solutions to every situation." This was especially good news to Farhad when his face was pinned to the mat by his practice partner's knee.

"In this situation," Pummeling Pete said to Farhad, whose ear that wasn't pinned to the mat was listening carefully, "the swing-pinner can turn his belly to the mat in a defensive position or call to the gentleman to take a short step backward, promenade, and twirl on his toe."

Farhad soon got a feel for this fast-growing sport. There was a lot to it. Right from the sound of the sharp crack of the starting gun, a swing-pinner could bow to his or her partner and do-si-do or bring him or her forcibly to the mat with an arm-lock hip throw. He liked choosing between a sagging body-lock throw (which was a favorite of Olympic wrestler Andy Seras and was perfected by swing-pinner and three-time blue ribbon winner in the Serenac County Fair buttermilk biscuit bake off Laurie Sue Johnson) and the buzz swing performed to the tune of "Polly Wolly Doodle." Either solution was equally correct.

One day while he lay cheek down on the mat with his own heel pressed into his ear and held tight by a muscular swing-pin practice partner in a powder blue square dance dress, Farhad thought, "This is a lot like quadratic equations." Now, at first blush, this may sound like merely the mad ravings of a beginning-level swing-pinner with his heel in his ear, but in fact, quadratic equations also may have two possible solutions. Here are two now. Solve them.

A. $(x - 4)(2x + 1) = 0$

B. $x^2 - 6x = 40$

You Can't Keep Slope Down by Faye Nisonoff Ruopp and Paula Poundstone (Heinemann: Portsmouth, NH), © 2007.

Extra! Extra!

Extra Patterns, Relations, and Algebra problems are recommended for the treatment of anxiety caused by the mere sight of Patterns, Relations, and Algebra problems. If the condition persists, get plenty of rest and do more Patterns, Relations, and Algebra problems.

1. **State whether the following relationships between x and y might be linear, quadratic, or exponential:**

A. $y = 3x$

B.

INPUT, X	OUTPUT, Y
1	2
2	5
3	10
4	17
5	26

C.

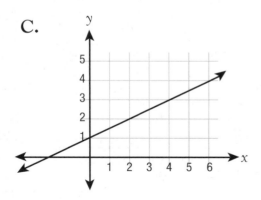

2. Find the slope of the line in part C of question 1.

3. Find the equation of a line with slope $\frac{2}{3}$ and y-intercept -8.

4. Add the following polynomials: $(3x^3 + 4x^2 - 7x + 11) + (-5x^2 + 9x - 7)$.

5. Multiply the following binomials: $(6s - 7)(3s + 1)$.

6. Solve the following quadratic equation: $x^2 = x + 42$.

Teacher Notes

1. Do Math, Get Gas

In problem 1, students are given tables, graphs, descriptions in words, and equations that represent either a linear, a quadratic, or an exponential relationship between two variables. Looking first at the tables given in parts A and C, it is helpful to examine any patterns in the output values.

In part A, the outputs increase by 3 as the inputs increase by 1; therefore, the relationship is *linear*. If the second differences (the differences between the differences in the outputs) were constant, the relationship would be *quadratic*.

In part C, the outputs are not increasing by a constant amount; the difference between the first two outputs $(2 - 1)$ is 1; the difference between the second and third outputs $(4 - 2)$ is 2; between the third and fourth $(8 - 4)$ is 4. Now let's examine the second differences (the differences between the differences: the difference between 2 and 1, 4 and 2, etc.); they, too, are not constant. Further examination will demonstrate that the third differences are not constant as well. It is helpful at this point to look at the outputs and think about a multiplicative relationship: is there a number that is a constant multiplier to get from one output to the next? In fact, the values are doubling. The constant multiplier is 2. Relationships with constant multipliers that produce outputs are *exponential*. As an extension, ask students if they can find an equation of the relationship defined by this table.

In part B, students are given the graph of a relationship between x and y that is a parabola.

Parabolas are graphical representations of *quadratic* relationships. In this case, each output is 1 more than the square of each input. Squaring represents a quadratic relationship, and therefore the equation defined in part E is also *quadratic*. In part D, a constant rate of 3 meters per second defines a *linear* relationship. Similar to the table in part A, there will be a constant difference in outputs of 3.

Students will examine linear, quadratic, exponential, trigonometric, and other nonlinear functions in future mathematics courses. As an extension, ask students to draw the graph of a function where each output is obtained by tripling the previous input.

2. You Can't Keep Slope Down

For problem 2, students need to be able to find the slope of a line given its equation (part A) and its graph (part B). If a linear equation is written in the form $y = mx + b$ (this is known as the slope-intercept form), then the coefficient of x (which is m) is the slope of the line. Therefore, the slope of this line is -3. Lines with negative slope slant downward when moving from left to right. As an extension, ask students to research why the letter m is used for slope. They may be surprised at the answer!

For part B, students should first observe that the line has a positive slope, which can be deduced from the observation that it slants upward when moving from left to right. To find the value of the slope, students might first pick two points on the line whose coordinates are easy to determine. Two points might be (0, 2) and (1, 5). There are several ways to find the slope of a line given two points. Using the graph, have students use a finger to travel from (0, 2) to (1, 5) by starting at (0, 2), first moving horizontally 1 unit to the right, and then moving vertically 3 units up. Slope is defined as rise (vertical change) over run (horizontal change); therefore, the slope is $\frac{3}{1}$ or 3.

Some students may know the formula for finding the slope between two points (x_1, y_1) and (x_2, y_2)

$$\text{slope} = \frac{(y_2 - y_1)}{(x_2 - x_1)}$$

Using this formula, with the first point (0, 2) and second point (1, 5), the slope is:

$$\frac{(5 - 2)}{(1 - 0)} \text{ or } \frac{3}{1}, \text{ or } 3$$

When students study calculus, they will discover that not all functions have constant slopes. As an extension, ask students to draw two different lines with slope $-\frac{4}{3}$. What is true about these lines?

3. Graphing to Blow Their Tops Off

To solve problem 3, students again need to know the meaning of the constants m and b in the general equation of the line $y = mx + b$. Since m is the slope of the line, and b is the y-intercept, the line will have a slope of ⁻2 and y-intercept of 3. To sketch the graph, first locate the y-intercept, three units above the origin on the y-axis. From this point, consider what a slope of ⁻2 means. It may be helpful to write ⁻2 in fractional form: $\frac{-2}{1}$.

This ratio represents rise over run. Start at (0, 3), the y-intercept. Since the numerator is negative, move down 2. You should now be at (0, 1). Since

the run is positive, move right 1 unit. You should now be at (1, 1). The following illustration demonstrates how to draw the line with this slope:

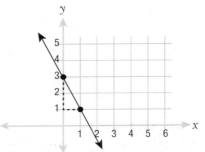

The answer to part B is that ⁻2 represents the slope of the line, and 3 represents the point (0, 3), where the line crosses the y-axis, or the y-intercept. As an extension, have students draw a line with slope 0 and y-intercept (0, 4). What is true about lines with slope 0?

4. Like Terms Are No Joke

Problem 4 asks students to add, subtract, and multiply polynomials. In order to add and subtract polynomials (parts A and B), students need to think about like terms (terms with the same variable raised to the same exponent) in algebraic expressions. For part A, it might be helpful to group like terms before adding:

$$(x^2 + {}^{-}2x^2) + (3x + 5x) + ({}^{-}7 + {}^{-}3)$$

The answer is

$${}^{-}x^2 + 8x + {}^{-}10, \text{ or } {}^{-}x^2 + 8x - 10$$

When working on part B, it may be helpful to write the subtraction problem as an addition problem by adding the opposite of the second expression:

$$(6n^2 + 4n - 7) + {}^{-}(2n^2 - 5n + 1)$$

We can then take the opposite of each term in the second expression

$$(6n^2 + 4n - 7) + ({}^{-}2n^2 + 5n - 1)$$

Now we can group like terms, as we did in part A:

$$(6n^2 + {}^-2n^2) + (4n + 5n) + ({}^-7 + {}^-1)$$

The answer is $4n^2 + 9n - 8$.

To solve part C, students need to multiply two binomials. One way to think about this is to use the distributive property twice: first to distribute $3r$ through $({}^-2r + 1)$ and then to distribute $^-5$ through $({}^-2r + 1)$. In other words:

$$(3r - 5)({}^-2r + 1) = 3r({}^-2r + 1) + {}^-5({}^-2r + 1)$$

Simplifying, we have

$$^-6r^2 + 3r + 10r - 5, \text{ or } {}^-6r^2 + 13r - 5$$

Some students may remember the mnemonic FOIL (*first, outer, inner, last*), representing the order in which we can think about multiplying. Look at each binomial separately.

- *First* refers to the first term in each binomial, or $3r$ and ^-2r. Multiplying these, we have $3r \times {}^-2r$, or $^-6r^2$.

- *Outer* refers to the terms that are to the far left and right, or $3r$ and 1. Multiplying these, we have $3r \times 1$, or $3r$.

- *Inner* refers to the two innermost terms, $^-5$ and ^-2r; multiplying these, we have $^-5 \times {}^-2r$, or $10r$.

- *Last* refers to the two last terms in each binomial, or $^-5$ and 1; multiplying these, we have $^-5 \times 1$, or $^-5$.

- The sum of these four products is $^-6r^2 + 3r + 10r + {}^-5$, or $^-6r^2 + 13r - 5$.

In fact, FOIL defines the same process as using the distributive property twice. As an extension, ask students to find the two binomials that when multiplied together produce $12x^2 + x - 6$.

5. Bow to Your Partner and Squish 'Im Flat

Problem 5 asks students to solve quadratic equations given in different forms. In part A, the quadratic is given in factored form. Students should notice that the equation represents multiplying two binomials whose product is 0. If the product of two numbers is 0, one or both of the numbers must be 0. Therefore, we need to find values of x that make the value of each binomial 0.

If $(x - 4) = 0$, then x must equal 4.

If $(2x + 1) = 0$, then x must equal $^-\frac{1}{2}$.

Therefore, the two solutions to this quadratic equation are 4 and $^-\frac{1}{2}$. If students are not convinced, have them substitute these values back into the original equation one at a time to find the result.

In part B, students are given another quadratic equation, but it is not in a form that is easily solved using either factoring or the quadratic formula. In order to use the same method as we used in part A, we need to set the quadratic expression equal to 0. Therefore, a first step might be to subtract 40 from each side, which results in the equation $x^2 - 6x - 40 = 0$. The next step is to determine if we can factor the quadratic trinomial (three terms) on the left. In fact, the quadratic factors into $(x - 10)(x + 4)$. Therefore the equation becomes $(x - 10)(x + 4) = 0$. The solutions are $x = 10$ and $x = {}^-4$.

To check these answers, students can substitute these values back into the original equation to see if they work. If students do not notice that this quadratic can be factored, they can also use the quadratic formula to solve this quadratic, or any quadratic in the form $ax^2 + bx + c = 0$, where a, b, and c are constants, and $a \neq 0$. The quadratic formula states that if $ax^2 + bx + c = 0$, then

$$x = \frac{^-b \pm \sqrt{b^2 - 4ac}}{2a}$$

For this problem, $a = 1$, $b = {}^-6$, and $c = {}^-40$. Substituting these numbers into the formula, we find that

$$x = \frac{^-({}^-6) \pm \sqrt{({}^-6)^2 - 4(1)({}^-40)}}{2(1)}$$

You Can't Keep Slope Down by Faye Nisonoff Ruopp and Paula Poundstone (Heinemann: Portsmouth, NH), © 2007.

Simplifying, we get $x = \dfrac{6 \pm \sqrt{36 + 160}}{2}$

or $\dfrac{6 \pm \sqrt{196}}{2}$, or $\dfrac{6 \pm 14}{2}$.

The two solutions are $\dfrac{6 + 14}{2}$, or $\dfrac{20}{2}$, or 10, and $\dfrac{6 - 14}{2}$, or $\dfrac{-8}{2}$, or -4.

Factoring first is clearly easier! However, not all quadratics factor, and therefore knowing the quadratic formula is certainly helpful. As an extension, ask students to find a quadratic equation whose solutions are 5 and $\dfrac{-3}{4}$.

Extra! Extra!

1. A. exponential; B. quadratic; C. linear
2. $\dfrac{1}{2}$
3. $y = \dfrac{2}{3}x - 8$
4. $3x^3 - x^2 + 2x + 4$
5. $18s^2 - 15s - 7$
6. $x = 7$ or $x = -6$

Geometry

The problems that follow are in the Geometry strand. The mathematics in these problems focuses on the concepts of congruence and similarity and transformations in the Cartesian coordinate plane. Students in grades 8 and 9 explore the angles formed by parallel lines cut by a transversal, and applications of the Pythagorean Theorem.

The topics covered in these problems were chosen from state and national standards:

- Classify figures in terms of congruence and similarity
- Understand the relationships of angles formed by parallel lines cut by a transversal
- Apply the Pythagorean Theorem
- Transform figures using translations, reflections, and rotations

Geometry

A Brilliant Fuss

Stunned by the intellect of Bartholemew the Baby Genius, people often make the mistake of forgetting that he is indeed a baby. He's a baby genius. When he gets tired, however, he's a cranky baby genius. Although he is well aware of the results of Harvard University's studies on sleep, when he gets a bit fussy and his mother tells him sympathetically, "Honey, you're tired," he wails, "Sleep plays important roles in physical growth, behavior, and emotional development and is closely related to cognitive functioning, learning, and attention in children, but not for me-e-e-e!"

On Friday night Bartholemew's parents stepped out to enjoy a wonderful meal at their favorite Italian restaurant and ended with an evening of lively swing dancing. Bartholemew enjoyed the company of Martha, his sixteen-year-old baby-sitter, but he ended the evening screaming in his crib, doing a lively dance of his own.

Most of the night went great. Bartholemew disassembled and rewired his Little Fella Fone 'n' Fun into the doorbell so that when someone rang the bell at the front door, the high-pitched recorded voice of Freddy Fun Fella would blare, "Hey, little fella! Thanks for being my friend!"

After she gave him a bath with his favorite blue whale sponge, popped him in a clean, fresh diaper, and snaked his doughy baby feet into his footy pajamas, Martha even let Bartholemew stay up past his bedtime to help with her math homework.

You Can't Keep Slope Down by Faye Nisonoff Ruopp and Paula Poundstone (Heinemann: Portsmouth, NH), © 2007.

Unfortunately, it may have been a bit too late for Bartholemew to stay up. When Martha lowered him into his crib, he began to kick his little feet and scream, "I want my blue square pattern block!" Martha quickly scanned the floor for a blue square pattern block and offered it to him. Grabbing the block while doing something that looked like a violent rain dance, Bartholemew yelled, "I need another one!" As fast as she could, Martha grabbed another pattern block and handed it to her screaming charge. Half a second later, the pattern blocks came flying out of the crib to Bartholemew's wail of "They're not congruent!"

"They're both blue!" shouted Martha, taking cover behind the rocking chair. She tried a great variety of pattern blocks before he wound down and fell over in a sound sleep. She thought she'd put a pair of congruent pattern blocks on his felt board so he could see it when he woke up, knowing now how much it meant to him, but she still didn't know what *congruent* meant. She sure didn't want to go through that again; it was already pouring rain out.

In each of the following problems, decide whether figures I and II are congruent. Explain how you know. Tell Martha.

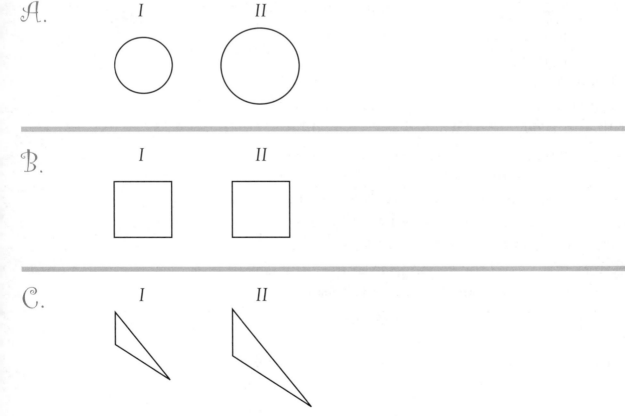

You Can't Keep Slope Down by Faye Nisonoff Ruopp and Paula Poundstone (Heinemann: Portsmouth, NH), © 2007.

Geometry

How Rude!

Gina wasn't invited to a lot of parties. She was quite good at math. That was something, of course. She knew all about quadratic equations, enjoyed the heck out of exponents, and spent most of her free time thinking about the distributive property, but she didn't have much in the way of manners.

Even at this year's Math Lovers' Ball she put people off a bit. She burped her multiplication tables, which some people did think was funny the first time she did it, less so the second and third times, and not at all by the fourth.

During the program she was especially rude. When one of the founders of the twenty-year-old Math Lovers' Ball approached the podium to receive an award, Gina said a bit too loudly under her breath, "I've got year-old cream cheese in my refrigerator that looks fresher than this guy." And when the renowned Dr. Lonnie Beckman read from his moving book, *When One Is Not Enough*, about his breakthrough work helping young people who can't stop doing math, she called him Yawnie and kept making exaggerated yawning gestures.

She cut in line at the buffet table. She said she was intersecting. She licked the serving spoon from the garlic mashed potatoes and put it back, and she said the beans looked like they'd been used already.

When she got to the beautifully decorated sheet cake with rectangular 2 cm by 5 cm slices, she grabbed

You Can't Keep Slope Down by Faye Nisonoff Ruopp and Paula Poundstone (Heinemann: Portsmouth, NH), © 2007.

the cake cutter and sliced her own piece with dimensions twice the length of each side of the other slices. Seeing the appalled look on the face of the math lover behind her in line, Gina said, "What? It's similar to the other servings!"

Draw a rectangle with dimensions 2 cm by 5 cm. Now draw another rectangle with dimensions twice the length of each side.

Well, was Gina's serving similar to the original servings? How do you know? Was it mannerly to take it?

3 Geometry

Problem

A Tail of Fine Art

You are spending your Saturday afternoon taking in the sights and sounds of the Art Barn. It's a huge place swarming with art, art collectors, and art dealers hoping to make a deal, find a treasure, or simply purchase a canvas big enough to cover up the hole the surfboard put in the wall in the living room that won't clash with the couch, no matter what is painted on it.

There are paintings of everything imaginable. There are paintings of cars, flowers, and fruit, both fresh and rotten. There are paintings of ballerinas, torn baseballs, boxers, babies, and the imaginary compartments inside a teenager's brain. There are paintings of tear-stained faces lifted in prayer, paintings of dogs playing cards, and paintings of half-naked women. There are paintings of half-naked card-playing dogs with their tear-stained faces lifted in prayer.

You happen to spot your kind elderly neighbor, Ms. Sweetchins, with her constant canine companion, Mr. Señor. Mr. Señor is, in fact, a rather fat dachshund, but because Ms. Sweetchins believes he barks in Spanish, she adoringly calls him Mr. Señor. Ms. Sweetchins is a woman of modest means, but whatever she has she splits 20/80 with Mr. Señor, and he has the sunglasses, doggie beds, rhinestone leashes, and carpeted moveable stairs to the couch to prove it.

Today Mr. Señor sits at Ms. Sweetchins' feet, wearing a sombrero and a bolo tie, looking worried while she excitedly shows a painting of two orange triangles to a

You Can't Keep Slope Down by Faye Nisonoff Ruopp and Paula Poundstone (Heinemann: Portsmouth, NH), © 2007.

very tall modern-art dealer wearing thick brown lipstick and huge triangular painted-on eyebrows.

"Mr. Señor found it in my attic. He often goes through my things looking for chew toys," Ms. Sweetchins tells the art dealer. "And Mr. Señor and I are practically certain that it's an original Zino Blotto painting."

"A Zino Blotto! That could be worth thousands," the art dealer shouts, grabbing the canvas. "Yes, it could be," she says, inspecting it closely. "There's only one way to tell. Zino Blotto's triangles were always similar."

"Are these triangles similar?" asks Ms. Sweetchins. "I do hope so. Mr. Señor would like to buy a cell phone, and he'd like to have lots of features on it."

"Well, I don't know. I studied art, not geometry. Are there any geometry experts in the barn?" the art dealer begins to shout urgently. You stride over, chest puffed out with pride in your knowledge of geometry, and figure out if the triangles (shown in the illustration) are similar.

Are they? Can Mr. Señor afford a cell phone with an unlimited calling plan? How do you know?

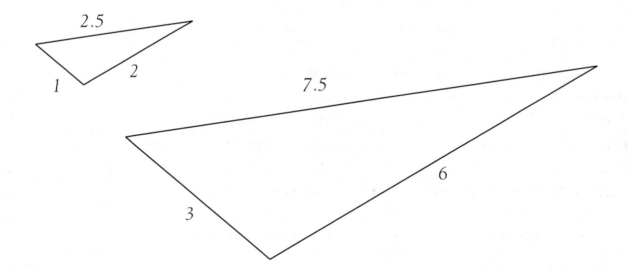

Choking on Geometry

It's the dream of many a young person to play some-day for the California Angels. However, because of a misprint on his dream form, Leonardo Digit got an opportunity to play for the California Angles, a geometry team.

Despite a potentially career-ending injury in his first game ever, Leonardo was now in his third sea-son with the California Angles. Today's game against the Hillsboro Hypotenuses was brutal. It was about 105° out there on that field, which made it espe-cially hard to calculate degrees of angle measurement. Nothing seemed to be going well for the Angles today. They didn't want to be unsportsmanly, but it did some-times seem that there may have been some favoritism on the part of the game's officials. Eric Schlutzgy got clob-bered by a "Find the area of a polygon" question and Daisy Billington had a "Calculate the angle of a pizza slice" question in which she was told only that its top-pings were sausage and black olives. Whereas the Hillsboro Hypotenuses were lobbed "Which of these two shapes is a square?" questions, more than once. On top of that, the Angles made lots of careless errors.

"What's going on out there?" Coach Rhombus asked his dejected Angles in the locker room at halftime. Coach Rhombus cared a lot about geometry. It was only his wife's threat to file curves in all of his rulers that stopped him from naming his son Pythagoras. "You guys

You Can't Keep Slope Down by Faye Nisonoff Ruopp and Paula Poundstone (Heinemann: Portsmouth, NH), © 2007.

are missing the point here. What are you doing with all of the formulas and rules we've practiced? Saving them for Mother's Day? Use them now! Your mothers will be happy with a nice card and a clean bathroom. Now, get out there, invert those attitudes, use those formulas and rules, and win!"

The Angles took the field with renewed hope, made a remarkable comeback, and tied up the score, but in the last play of the game Leonardo got slammed by a two-part question and choked. His teammates began to shout mostly positive things at him. The crowd began to shout some positive things at him, but Leonardo just stood there with a dazed look, making small movements in the air with his pencil as if he were conducting a teeny, tiny orchestra. The coach could tell he was in trouble, so he called a time-out and ran some water out to Leonardo on the field.

"OK, Leonardo, what's the question?" Coach Rhombus asked.

"This is terrible. I hate angle questions."

"That's the question?" asked Coach Rhombus, surprised.

"No," said Leonardo, "it's got two parts: A. Find the measures of angles a, b, c, d, e, f, g, h, i, j, k, m, n, and o, in the figure; and B. Is line l_3 parallel to line l_4? Why or why not?"

"I can't do that. That's not one question. That's an interview, an inquisition, a lifetime of research!"

"Calm down," Coach Rhombus counseled. "Here's your water."

"Hey, someone drank my water," complained Leonardo.

"How do you know?" asked Coach Rhombus.

"Because I know how much I had before. Hey, that's it, Coach Rhombus. I can do it now! I can find the measures of the angles. I know a straight angle formed by a line is 180°. If I know what I start with, I can figure out what's missing."

With that, Leonardo banged out the measures of angles a, b, c, d, e, f, g, h, i, j, k, m, n, and, o, and determined whether or not the lines were parallel to bring in the winning score.

Before he knew it, Leonardo was lifted into the air by the combined strength of the California Angles and their fans. As he flew over Coach Rhombus' head, he emptied the rest of his water onto it and yelled, "Thank you, coach!"

"You're welcome, Leonardo," answered the coach. "Hydration is a very important part of geometry."

You Can't Keep Slope Down by Faye Nisonoff Ruopp and Paula Poundstone (Heinemann: Portsmouth, NH), © 2007.

A.   Take a look at this figure and find the measures of angles *a*, *b*, *c*, *d*, *e*, *f*, *g*, *h*, *i*, *j*, *k*, *m*, *n*, and *o*, just like Leonardo did. Be sure to drink lots of water.

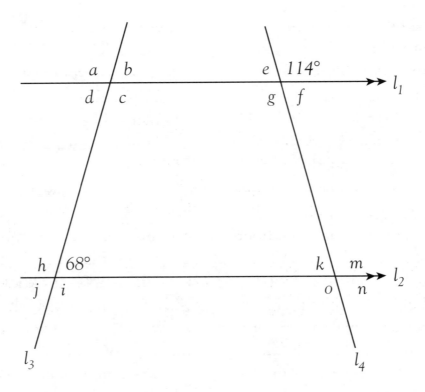

B.   Take another swig of H_2O and figure out if line l_3 is parallel to line l_4.

Show-Stopping Geometry

The Great Zamboni was a fabulous showman. The circus was, as they say, in his blood. If the Great Zamboni's World-Famous Circus was no longer the spectacular heart-stopping extravaganza it had once been, you wouldn't know it from the Great Zamboni's ringmaster oratory. He still drew the crowd to the edge of their seats with anticipation during his rousing introductions. Unfortunately, as of late, the acts themselves did not keep the crowd on the edge of their seats, but rather slouched in their seats, even able to break into small discussion groups about the weather and where might the world have been without Velcro.

The human cannonball was just a guy in a helmet who was thrust from behind a curtain by some clowns. After a riveting preamble by the Great Zamboni about the daring, death-defying feats of the human projectile, there were loud grunting sounds followed shortly by a thud.

The savvy entertainment-goer may have been tipped off that the Great Zamboni was filling in for a few of the performers by the long pause between his introduction of them and their appearance. The duct tape was coming loose from the ends of the snake charmer's turban wrap, and the snake, which looked suspiciously like a garden hose with a happy face drawn on it, was unresponsive.

The clown car in most circuses is a tiny vehicle that zips into the spotlight and unloads a seemingly endless stream of clowns, leaving the audience scratching their heads, wondering how so many could fit, especially considering the size of their shoes. The Great Zamboni's World-Famous Circus clown car was an old bus. There were only three clowns inside and they had plenty of legroom.

The show had been losing an acrobat per show because of a flaw in the grand finale. Tonight the Great Zamboni himself would star in the grand finale. A muscle-bound acrobat in a sea green leotard proudly stepped into the center ring with a chair on the top of his head. He was tossed another chair, which he caught upon the first, followed by another and another and another, until he balanced a stack of chairs 15 ft. high into the air. The roustabouts then anchored a 15 ft. ladder to the floor 3 ft. from the tower of chairs. Some more bulgy musclemen in sea green leotards held the ladder straight up and steady while the Great Zamboni climbed to a platform on the top, where he sat with a flourish and shrugged, as if to say, "That couldn't have been easier," and waited with a "Tada!" on the tip of his tongue for the ladder to be leaned to the chair tower, where he would slide gracefully onto the top chair amidst the roar of the approving crowd.

Instead, he came to in a hospital bed beside the acrobat who suffered the same fate during the earlier matinee performance.

What was wrong with the Great Zamboni's World-Famous Circus' grand finale?

Think of it this way: How high up a wall will a 15 ft. ladder reach if the foot of the ladder is 3 ft. from the wall?

On Second Thought, Go Ahead and Huff and Puff

Everything was happy hooves and satisfied snouts in the immediate aftermath of the three little pigs' successful bamboozling of the big bad wolf. However, relations among the pigs within the sturdy brick dwelling became a bit strained in the weeks that followed. The sensible pig, who cleverly built the brick house to ward off the wolf, never actually said, "I told you so," to his less nose-to-the-grindstone brothers, whose poorly planned, flimsy stick and straw residences were almost no obstacle at all to the huff and puff of the wolf, but the unspoken words seemed to take up space in the air around them. The stick-house pig and the straw-house pig had a sense that they'd be known hereafter as the not-so-bright pigs, and this thought did nothing to motivate them. They didn't appear to be making plans to go anywhere, and the brick-house pig began to wonder when they might.

The brick-house pig lived a carefully ordered life. He changed the vacuum cleaner bag every other Tuesday. After a brisk walk around the neighborhood each morning, he quickly cleaned the doorknobs. The straw-house pig and the stick-house pig tended to sleep in, and the brick-house pig often had to dust around them. They left potato skins on the floor and moved the furniture to play football in the living room. They were less than tidy in the bathroom, and when the brick-house pig placed fresh-cut flowers there to overcome the stench, they ate them. The once roomy brick house had become a bit tight.

After about a month the homeowner dropped the hammer. He told the straw-house pig and the stick-house pig that from that moment on, "just hanging out" could be scratched off their daily planners, to which they replied, "What's a daily planner?" Their brick-house brother made the two slacker pigs clean the crumbs out of the toaster oven every morning, whether they toasted or not, "just to be on the safe side." They had to take down their skateboarding posters and scrape the tape off of the wall. The straw-house pig and the stick-house pig began to wonder if escaping from the wolf was such a lucky break after all.

Today, when the brick-house pig woke his brothers at 6:00 A.M. to tell them that they had to rotate every piece of furniture in the living room 30° around the point of the mustard stain on the rug before he returned from his power walk, they stuck their heads out the window and called, "Here, wolfie, wolfie," as soon as the brick-house pig was out of earshot. They don't know the first thing about angles of rotation. They can't even control their mustard. Come help them. Show them this problem as an example:

What is the angle of rotation if triangle *ABC* is rotated about point *P* to form the image triangle *DEF*? You will need a protractor to answer this. If you don't have one, make a reasonable estimate.

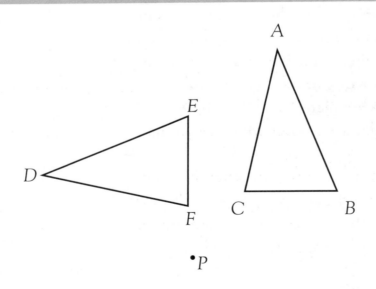

Bird Brains

"Raise your wing if you've ever bonked into a building before," bellowed an enormous pigeon standing before a large gathering of young birds on the library steps. The little tweets quickly darted looks back and forth at one another. One or two birds started to lift and then quickly lower their wings, reluctant to reveal anything that another bird hadn't.

"Nothing to be ashamed of. It happens," said the big pigeon, surveying the crowd. "That's why you're here at Captain Fuss N. Feathers' safety school. It's not enough to rely on instinct in a world full of skyscrapers, airplanes, wedding rice, and plastic six-pack holders."

Captain Fuss N. Feathers held up a picture of a propeller. "Can anyone tell me what this is?" he asked.

"Lots of twirling wings!" chirped a little bird with a bald spot on its crest.

"No! No! No!" shouted Captain Fuss N. Feathers. "It is not. It is a dangerous man machine that can knock the feathers right off a bird's head or worse."

"Oh," chorused the little birds gravely.

"How about this?" asked the captain, holding up a picture of an airplane.

"It's my great grandpa!" called out a delighted sturdy little bird.

"No! It's not!" shouted Captain Fuss N. Feathers. "Do any of your family members leave a trail of smoke and have wheels?"

You Can't Keep Slope Down by Faye Nisonoff Ruopp and Paula Poundstone (Heinemann: Portsmouth, NH), © 2007.

"Well, I haven't met them all," said the little bird, looking injured.

"It's no wonder flightless animals like cats can catch us," said Captain Fuss N. Feathers, burying his head under his wing miserably. "Now pay attention. What is this?" He held a large mirror in front of his foul students.

"Friends!" they peeped and flapped excitedly.

"We're gonna lose the whole species," mumbled the captain. "No, it's a mirror. The birds you see in it are your own reflections. Each point on your little bird bodies is as far from the mirror as is the reflected point. So when you are close enough to kiss what you thought was your friend, you are about to smack into the mirror."

"Oh," came the nasal-sounding response of a little bird with a smushed-in beak.

Captain Fuss N. Feathers was ready to peck out his own brains. Perhaps you could illustrate the idea and show it to young birds you meet in the future.

Here is a drawing of a figure and a line of reflection. Draw the figure's reflection over this line.

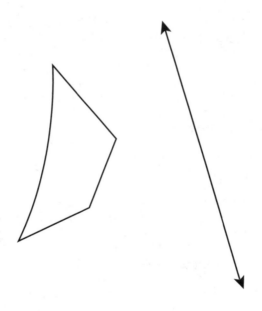

How Do We Get Rid of All of This Good 'n' Yummy Macaroni and Cheese?

Gloriosa was rather disappointed by her first professional acting experience, a commercial for Good 'n' Yummy macaroni and cheese, in which she played a child who was delighted with her serving of Good 'n' Yummy macaroni and cheese.

Making a commercial was an incredibly slow process. Lots of people worked on it and they argued endlessly about every detail.

"She should use a spoon."

"Studies show fork users buy more macaroni."

"The macaroni and cheese box should be on the table. Studies show spoon eaters keep the box on the table."

"She should wear a green shirt."

"She should wear a pink shirt."

"She shouldn't be eating alone. She looks like a loser."

"Studies show losers eat a lot of macaroni and cheese."

"Her hair should be bigger."

"Only losers in pink shirts buy lots of macaroni and cheese."

"What study are you talking about?"

"OK, there was no study. I just thought about it a lot."

Gloriosa was supposed to sit at a table in front of a bowl of Good 'n' Yummy macaroni and cheese and say, "Thanks, Mom, you're the best mom in the whole world! When I eat a bowl of super-deee-licious Good 'n' Yummy macaroni and cheese I feel like I'm eating a wedge of farm-fresh cheese the size of me!" Then she was supposed to take a bite and look as though her life had improved immeasurably. The camera was to pull back to reveal a towering triangular cheese wedge, the sight of which was to both surprise and amuse Gloriosa.

Of course, what she wanted to say was that if you ate a wedge of cheese the size of yourself, the size of yourself would double and that would be only half of your problem. Not to mention that there's not a mom alive who wants to be valued for the kind of macaroni and cheese she purchases. But Gloriosa kept her thoughts to herself.

Everyone had a different opinion about where the cheese wedge should be located, so the set designer plotted the cheese wedge on a graph and poor Gloriosa was stuck doing retake after retake with the vertices of the triangular cheese wedge moving point by point around the set. She wasn't sure she could smile at one more noodle, yummy or not, but she knew for sure she never wanted to star in a movie about macaroni and cheese.

A.   In the last take, the triangle had vertices (-3, 3), (1, 4), and (-1, 2). If the triangle were translated 2 units to the right and 5 units down, what would the coordinates of its image be?

B.   If the original triangle in part A were reflected over the *x*-axis, what would the coordinates of its image be?

You Can't Keep Slope Down by Faye Nisonoff Ruopp and Paula Poundstone (Heinemann: Portsmouth, NH), © 2007.

Extra! Extra!

You say you've done enough geometry? You may have a point, but if you can't measure the angles formed by two lines that intersect, then a bit more work along that line couldn't hurt.

1. Draw two congruent quadrilaterals. How do you know they are congruent?

2. The dimensions of one rectangle are 3 cm by 5 cm. A second rectangle has dimensions 7 cm by 9 cm. Are the rectangles similar? Why or why not?

3. Find the values of angles *a, b, c, d, e, f,* and *g* in the following drawing:

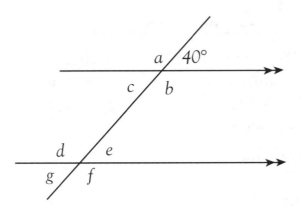

4. Find the length of the hypotenuse in the following right triangle:

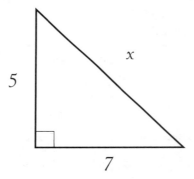

5. Rotate the following triangle 180° about point **R**.

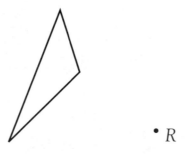

You Can't Keep Slope Down by Faye Nisonoff Ruopp and Paula Poundstone (Heinemann: Portsmouth, NH), © 2007.

6. In the following drawing, *A'B'C'D'* is the reflection of *ABCD* over a line. Find and draw the line of reflection.

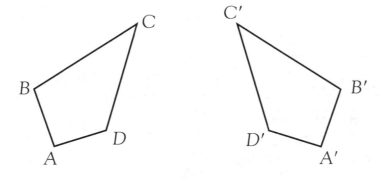

7. A. A triangle with vertices (1, 5), (3, 2), and (⁻4, 1) is translated 3 units to the left and 1 unit up. Find the coordinates of the vertices of its image.

   B. The triangle in part A is reflected over the y-axis. What are the coordinates of the vertices of its image?

Geometry

Teacher Notes

1. A Brilliant Fuss

For problem 1, students need to know the definition of congruent figures: figures that are the same size and the same shape. We can determine whether the pairs of figures in parts A, B, and C are congruent by inspection. The two circles in part A are different sizes; therefore, they are not congruent. Likewise, the two triangles in part C are different sizes, and are not congruent. The two squares in part B appear to be the same size, and therefore they are most likely congruent. One way to determine if the squares in part B are congruent is to cut one out and overlay it on the other to see if they coincide. For these problems, using informal methods of determining congruence is appropriate. As an extension, ask students if all squares are congruent.

2. How Rude!

For problem 2, students are asked to draw the two rectangles, one with dimensions 2 cm by 5 cm, and another with dimensions 4 cm by 10 cm (twice the length of each side of the original):

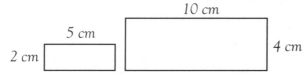

(Figures are not shown full size here.)

The rectangles are similar, since they both contain all right angles and therefore their corresponding angles are equal, and each pair of corresponding sides is in the same ratio, 1 to 2.

In general, figures are similar if they are the same shape, but not necessarily the same size. As an extension, ask students to draw two rectangles that are not similar.

3. A Tail of Fine Art

For problem 3, students need to determine if two triangles are similar. In general, two triangles are similar if their corresponding angles are equal and their corresponding sides are in the same ratio. Students will need a protractor to measure the angles in each triangle. In fact, the corresponding angles are equal. Although students may learn in later courses that the condition of corresponding angles being equal is sufficient to prove triangles are similar, they may not understand this concept at this point.

Have them look at the ratios of the corresponding sides as well: 1:3, 2:6, 2.5:7.5. Since these ratios are equivalent, the triangles are similar. In fact, either condition alone (corresponding sides are in the same ratio or corresponding angles are equal) is enough to prove that the triangles are similar. As an extension, ask students the following question: If two quadrilaterals have all pairs of corresponding sides in the same ratio, are they similar?

4. Choking on Geometry

For problem 4, students need to understand the relationship of angles formed by parallel lines (in

You Can't Keep Slope Down by Faye Nisonoff Ruopp and Paula Poundstone (Heinemann: Portsmouth, NH), © 2007.

this case, l_1 and l_2) cut by transversals (in this case, l_3 and l_4). To answer part A, looking first at lines l_1 and l_2 cut by transversal l_4, the 114° angle is a corresponding angle with angle m. Since parallel lines form equal corresponding angles when cut by a transversal, we know that angle m is also 114°. Angles f and n are also corresponding angles, and since angle f is the supplement of 114° (supplementary angles add to 180°), angle f must be 66°. Therefore, angle n is also 66°. Angle g forms a vertical pair with the original 114° angle, and since vertical angles are equal (vertical angles are pairs of angles formed by two intersecting lines), angle g is also 114°. Since angle g and angle o are corresponding angles, angle o is 114°. Angle f is equal to angle e (vertical angles again), and therefore since angle f is 66°, angle e is also 66°. Angles e and k are corresponding angles, and therefore angle k is 66°. Using the same process for transversal l_3 and parallel lines l_1 and l_2, we can determine that angles h, a, i, and c are 112°, and angles b, d, and j are 68°. As an extension, ask students to find the measures (in terms of x and y) of each angle in the drawing if the measure of the 114° angle is x and the measure of the 68° angle is y.

For part B, students need to determine if l_3 and l_4 are parallel. One way to prove lines are parallel is to show that a pair of corresponding angles is equal. If we look at l_2 as the transversal cutting l_3 and l_4, then angle m and the 68° angle would have to be equal, since they form a pair of corresponding angles. However, angle m is 114°. Therefore, the lines are not parallel. When students study geometry in high school, they will encounter theorems and their converses. There is a theorem in geometry that states that if two parallel lines are cut by a transversal, the corresponding angles are equal. The converse of this theorem is that if corresponding angles are equal when two lines are cut by a transversal, then the lines are parallel. As an extension, ask students this question: What is the converse of the Pythagorean Theorem?

5. Show-Stopping Geometry

For problem 5, students should make a sketch of the situation given, such as the following:

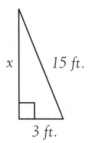

We need to find the value of x. Using the Pythagorean Theorem, since this is a right triangle, we can write the equation $x^2 + 3^2 = 15^2$. Simplifying, we obtain the equation $x^2 + 9 = 225$. Subtracting 9 from both sides, we have $x^2 = 216$, or $x = 14.7$ feet, rounded to the nearest tenth of a foot. As an extension, ask students to find as many Pythagorean triples as they can; in other words, find three whole numbers such that the sum of the squares of two of them is equal to the square of the third.

6. On Second Thought, Go Ahead and Huff and Puff

To find the angle of rotation for problem 6, students should connect points C and F (F is the image of C after the rotation) to the point of rotation, point P.

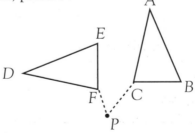

Now if we measure angle CPF, this will give us the angle of rotation. The measure of angle CPF is 45°. As an extension, ask students to draw the image of triangle ABC after it has been rotated 180° about point P.

7. Bird Brains

For problem 7, students need to draw the reflection of a figure over a line. A simple approach is to label the vertices of the figure, and reflect them over the line one at a time.

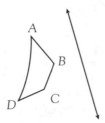

To reflect point A, draw a line segment from A perpendicular to the line of reflection.

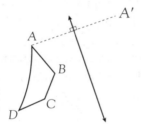

Extend this line segment an equal distance on the other side of the reflection line. Name this point A′, or the image of A. Repeat this process for points B, C, and D. The reflected figure should look like the following:

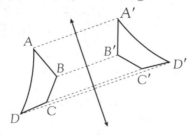

Together, the image A′B′C′D′ and the original figure ABCD form a figure with reflection symmetry. As an extension, ask students to find an object or figure in their house with reflection symmetry and to identify the line of reflection.

8. How Do We Get Rid of All of This Good 'n' Yummy Macaroni and Cheese?

To answer part A of question 8, students should first plot the three points on graph paper, as shown in the following:

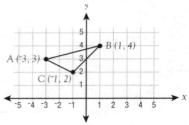

If the triangle is translated 2 units to the right, then each x-coordinate will be increased by 2. If the triangle is translated 5 units down, each y-coordinate will be decreased by 5. The image then will have coordinates (-1, -2), (3, -1), and (1, -3), as shown in the following sketch:

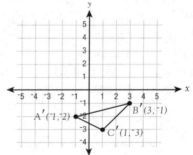

Algebraically, we can define this transformation as $(x, y) \rightarrow (x + 2, y - 5)$. As an extension, ask students to describe the transformation that will take the image constructed in this problem back to the original triangle.

For part B, students can think of reflecting each vertex of the triangle over the x-axis in a process similar to the one they used in problem 7. The result is shown in the following sketch:

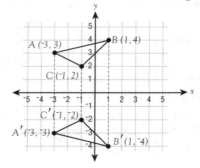

The coordinates of the image of ABC are A'(-3, -3), B'(1, -4), and C'(-1, -2). As an extension, ask students to generalize the results of a reflection over the x-axis: how would they describe the transformation of any point (x, y) under a reflection about the x-axis?

Extra! Extra!

1. Drawings will vary. The two quadrilaterals will be congruent if when one is placed on top of the other, they align. A more formal definition is that the two quadrilaterals will be congruent if their corresponding sides are equal and their corresponding angles are equal.

2. If the rectangles are similar, their corresponding sides will be in the same ratio. Since 3/7 is not equal to 5/9, the rectangles are not similar.

3. $a = 140°$, $b = 140°$, $c = 40°$, $d = 140°$, $e = 40°$, $f = 140°$, $g = 40°$.

4. $\sqrt{74}$

5.

6.

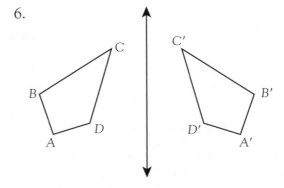

7. A. (-2, 6), (0, 3), (-7, 2)

    B. (-1, 5), (-3, 2), (4, 1)

You Can't Keep Slope Down by Faye Nisonoff Ruopp and Paula Poundstone (Heinemann: Portsmouth, NH), © 2007.

Measurement

The problems that follow are in the Measurement strand. The mathematics includes using proportions to convert among units of measurement between different systems (e.g., metric and customary). Students explore similarity and its relationship to scale factors. Students are also expected to determine the area and perimeter of two-dimensional figures such as parallelograms, trapezoids, and circles. In addition, students should be able to find the volume and surface area of prisms, cylinders, and spheres.

The topics covered in these problems were chosen from state and national standards:

- Convert from one system of measurement to another given the formulas

- Determine the area and perimeter or circumference of parallelograms, trapezoids, and circles

- Determine the surface area and volume of rectangular prisms, cylinders, and spheres

- Use ratio and proportion to solve problems involving similar figures

Lost Heart

Marcus was supposed to ride his bike 5,600 kilometers across the country for Habitat for Humanity, that wonderful group that builds houses for homeless people. If his sense of direction were anywhere near the size of his heart, it would have been a real success, too. One might think that when he gave a friendly wave and "Hi, how are you?" to the elderly Mrs. Gibbons, who sits out on her front porch at the house down on the end of his block, four days in a row, he might have had some idea that he was a bit off course. Still, Mrs. Gibbons enjoyed seeing him each and every time. He later said that he did notice that he saw Pete's Pizza Parlor four times, but hadn't realized it was the same one and had only felt happy for Pete that his business had grown so that he had opened three new restaurants.

Some people might have gotten a clue when they'd been riding for so many days that their legs continued to pump up and down even hours after they had dismounted their bike and were suffering from nearly fatal chafing, yet still had only one small New England state filled in on their license plate game. Those people, however, may not have volunteered the way Marcus did.

A couple of times he did get off of his bike and ask directions, but this only further confused him because people gave him directions in miles and he knew only how many kilometers he had to ride.

You Can't Keep Slope Down by Faye Nisonoff Ruopp and Paula Poundstone (Heinemann: Portsmouth, NH), © 2007.

In the end, Marcus did end up riding his bike 5,600 kilometers just looking for Habitat for Humanity. If 1 mile is about 1.6 kilometers, how many miles did he ride his bike?

Bride and Gloom

"Ms. Jane's Bridal World, everything the happy couple needs to make their special day the threshold to a lifetime of wedded bliss. Thiz Dave. How may I help you?" said Dave, answering the phone at his new job. The sound that came back through the phone at him was as unexpected as it was unidentifiable. It was a ghastly, guttural sob followed by a screech, tapering into a howl. At first, Dave wondered how an animal wounded all the way out in the Serengeti could get to a phone.

Then he thought he heard the words "bought a wedding dress," which really threw him because he'd never seen an animal in a wedding dress and couldn't imagine where it had gotten the cash for such a purchase. However, after the initial shock of the unpleasant sound had worn off, he realized that on the other end of the phone there was a very unhappy female customer. He thought he'd rather deal with the desperate call of a dying wildebeest.

"My wedding ceremony begins in thirty minutes, and when I took my wedding gown that I bought at your store from the box, there was a big red circle right on the front of the dress," the woman said, maintaining control with great effort.

"I'm sorry, ma'am, these things happen. Must have dropped a meatball on there at the rehearsal dinner," said Dave.

"I didn't wear it at the rehearsal dinner!" the woman shrieked, "I didn't want to get it dirty."

You Can't Keep Slope Down by Faye Nisonoff Ruopp and Paula Poundstone (Heinemann: Portsmouth, NH), © 2007.

"You should've. You'd have seen the stain earlier."

There was another odd noise on the line. Dave thought maybe she was gargling.

"The stain was on the dress when I took it from the box!"

"Oh, well," Dave said. "Hold on to it and eventually it'll be in style. If Brad Pittooey's wife wears it, everyone'll want one."

"I'm not planning on getting married again!" she yelled.

"Statistically, people do. Although, there's no record of divorce among couples where the bride wore a wedding dress with a big red circle on the front. So you've got that going for you."

"Look, are you going to help me or not?"

"I've already helped you. Marriage isn't perfect, you know? If you and your beloved can't weather the storm of a red circle on your wedding dress, you may as well call it off right now."

"I don't like your attitude."

"Look, lady, I'm pointing out a valuable life lesson practically for free. I'm very helpful, but OK, how big is the circle?"

"Its area is $100\,\pi$ cm^2."

"That's great, ma'am, but I'm gonna need the diameter and the circumference of the circle if I'm gonna help you further," Dave replied, but before he could finish the sentence, more animal noises came out of the phone.

Help Dave help the happy couple. Find each of the following, without using a calculator:

A. the diameter of the circle

B. the circumference of the circle

You Can't Keep Slope Down by Faye Nisonoff Ruopp and Paula Poundstone (Heinemann: Portsmouth, NH), © 2007.

Measurement

Howdy, Neighbor!

So, you're walking down the street and you hear some-one yell, "Let's get this helpful citizen to decide. Hey, you, come here a minute. Take a look at this," while waving a paper and motioning someone (apparently you) across the street to where he and another guy are in a heated argument. You look around, hoping that the person they really want is behind a bush nearby, and then slowly approach the two men. The guy waving the paper hands it to you. It bears the following figure, which shows the shape of a house lot for his property and the measurements of three of its sides on the plot plan.

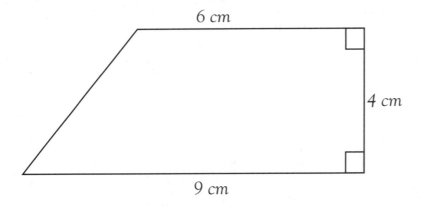

6 cm

4 cm

9 cm

Good fences make good neighbors, they say, but because of the missing measurement, these neighbors haven't been able to make that improvement in their relationship.

"My neighbor here, the human leaf blower, needs to know where exactly to build the edge of his cage," the other guy says while you're trying to study the diagram.

"What do you think of a neighbor who hangs his laundry outside?" he continues.

"Well, it does save electricity," you venture awkwardly.

"I'm not sure it's any of your business," the guy shoots back. "You wouldn't like it if your neighbor hung his big old boxers in the yard. They're so big, when the wind blows it sounds like someone's cracking a whip. I thought Siegfried and Roy were out there until I looked out the window. Then I thought it was a torn sail. I panicked. I thought we'd been attacked by pirates."

"Oh, yeah?" says the first guy, "well how would you like it if your neighbor sold your urn in his yard sale?"

"It was an accident!" the other neighbor yells in your ear, making it very difficult to concentrate on the dimensions of the plot.

"He says it was an accident," you mutter, hoping that your hearing comes back on that side someday.

"Yeah, I thought it was on my property, so I sold it, but I gave you the money."

"It had my mother's ashes in it! How can you defend this guy?" the first guy booms back, rounding on you.

Quick! Get yourself out of this no-win situation!

A. Find the length of the fourth side without measuring. I don't want to give too big a hint, but the initials of the theorem you need to use are Pythagorean.

B. If the scale on the plot plan is $\frac{1}{2}$ cm = 10 ft., find the perimeter of the lot.

C. Find the area of the lot. Make sure to include units.

D. Say you think you hear your mother calling and leave.

You Can't Keep Slope Down by Faye Nisonoff Ruopp and Paula Poundstone (Heinemann: Portsmouth, NH), © 2007.

Leonardo the Lifetime Learner and the Decimals of Doom

Leonardo Digit didn't know when he had ever felt so bad. He had thought he'd felt his worst a couple of days ago when his dad, Dick Digit, owner of Dick Digit's Number Depot—"where the whole family can shop for numbers and operations don't hurt a bit!"— had told him that he had to spend Friday night restocking shelves at the store instead of having a unicycle lesson with Twaddles the Clown, but this he realized definitely felt much worse.

Leonardo had had every intention of doing exactly what his dad had said, no matter how terribly unfair it was, but when Dick Digit had left for the evening to go to a business dinner to discuss a sponsorship deal with the "Math on Ice" show that was thrilling audiences everywhere, and Leonardo found himself alone with his thoughts, some of his not so well thought-out thoughts got the best of him. He was just arranging a shelf of exquisite glass 3's when it occurred to him that these shelves were the perfect height and distance apart from each other for beginning unicycling. Quickly, Leonardo placed a call to his friend and teacher, Twaddles the Clown, asking him to come that evening to Dick Digit's Number Depot to give him a unicycle lesson. Leonardo was absolutely planning to complete the work his father had asked him to do, so he feverishly opened boxes of complete sets of southwestern-style iron multiples of 10 through 100 and plastic baby-safe 1,000's until Twaddles' red nose showed up at the door.

You Can't Keep Slope Down by Faye Nisonoff Ruopp and Paula Poundstone (Heinemann: Portsmouth, NH), © 2007.

After that Leonardo lost all account of himself.

"I would have been here sooner," said Twaddles, catching his breath, "but I was in the backseat of the clown car. I had to wait for fifty clowns to get out before me."

They worked together at the "stepover," the safe way to dismount a unicycle, until Leonardo was falling down from the exhaustion of falling down. Twaddles, of course, reminded Leonardo repeatedly not to take his foot off the bottom pedal. Unicycle riding is not easy. Leonardo couldn't possibly learn it in one evening, but one thing he did learn is that if you try to learn unicycling anywhere near an enormous cylinder full of decimals, you might knock it over. He learned the hard way.

Leonardo lifted his face from a pile of pedals, spokes, and every kind of decimal a demanding public could love to purchase to see the huge cylinder, decorated with an appealing number pattern, scratched and dented, lying on its side. Even worse, his dad's face, bearing a disappointed expression, loomed above him.

"Dad, I was going to . . . I didn't mean to . . . I thought . . ." Leonardo stammered. His father just stared, speechless.

This, Leonardo thought, was definitely the worst he had ever felt. He clambored up from the floor. Twaddles began to juggle the displaced decimals, because he didn't always know when to juggle. "Twaddles is a great guy, but he'd juggle at a funeral," Leonardo thought and tried to signal him out with a jerk of his head toward the door.

"I'm sorry, Dad," said Leonardo. To his great relief, his father began, "Leonardo, my product, I was a smaller Digit myself once. I too made a certain percentage of mistakes. Even the best-intentioned among us sometimes forget which way to point our 'greater than, less than' sign. There's a great lesson to be learned here that you can carry with you and use throughout your life." Now Leonardo wasn't so sure he liked the sound of this. "And it is, of course, how to find the surface area of a cylinder. Toward that end, you will repair this one, calculate its surface area, and purchase the paint to paint the outside of it with a new appealing decorative number pattern."

Leonardo has no idea how to find the surface area of a cylinder. Show him how to do it.

Find the surface area of a cylinder if its height is 13 ft. and its volume is 325 π ft.[3]

You Can't Keep Slope Down by Faye Nisonoff Ruopp and Paula Poundstone (Heinemann: Portsmouth, NH), © 2007.

Up with Pins

"How many years you think we've been at this?" Sid, the one pin, asked Wanda, the two pin.

"I'll tell you after the sweep," she said, and their conversation paused as it always did while the rake swept them back to the pin-setting machine to be reset.

"You wanna get off me?" Sid said to Lester, the three pin, before they were loaded onto the pin elevator to be dropped into their proper place in the distributor.

"Sorry," mumbled Lester.

Two minutes later all of the pins were arranged neatly upright within a triangle shape with Sid at the forward-most point, while a bowler wiggled his sticky fingers into some holes in a ball, which he hoped to use to knock Sid and his nine coworkers down.

"Thirty maybe," said Wanda, finally replying to Sid's question. "I'm not sure. I'm not so good with numbers."

"Hold on, fellas!" shouted Sid. "This guy's got his name on his shirt and those aren't rental shoes he's wearing. They're the worst."

Sure enough, five seconds later, every pin lay face-down, awaiting the sweeper.

"Lester, you wanna get off me?" said Sid.

"Sorry," mumbled Lester.

"I don't know why you say that. You could total a score without a pencil long before they had computerized scoring," Sid continued to Wanda when they stood back in formation.

"Not again!" he shouted at the sight of the oncoming

You Can't Keep Slope Down by Faye Nisonoff Ruopp and Paula Poundstone (Heinemann: Portsmouth, NH), © 2007.

ball. All ten pins were bumped and shoved to a prone position.

"Yes, but you're really the brains of us pins. It was your idea to . . . I'll tell you after the sweep."

The pins were pushed unceremoniously to the pin elevator.

"Could you get off of me, Lester?" said Sid.

"Sorry," mumbled Lester.

". . . to kidnap the balls," said Wanda when she again stood tall behind Sid.

"Yeah, but it doesn't stop the game," said Sid dejectedly.

"It does temporarily, until the attendant comes out and retrieves them," Wanda persisted.

"Look how cool this guy thinks he is," said Sid, staring disgustedly down the alley at the bowler. "Like it's that hard to knock down ten pins with a ball that size. Hey, buddy! Why don't you stand your family up down here and I'll come up there and bowl?

"Uh-oh, here it comes!"

This time Sid took it right in the teeth, but when he looked up, there was Wanda still standing tall and proud.

"Honey, have you lost weight?" asked Sid.

"Sid," said Wanda in a worried voice after they were reset, "that ball is not regulation volume."

"How do you know?" asked Sid.

"Well, look at it. It looks like it's got a diameter of 6 inches, or a radius of 3 inches, right? So, what's its volume? Quickly, honey, we've gotta get this guy disqualified."

Help Sid. Find the volume of a sphere with a radius of 3 inches.

6 Measurement

Exactly Like a Bull in a China Shop

Gleeful at the prospect of a sale to a wealthy customer, Ms. Nellie sprang to her feet at the back of the store when she saw the enormous stretch limousine that rolled to a stop at the front door. She was quite surprised to see the passenger who disembarked, but later when she thought about it, she realized that it had been bound to happen eventually, what with the simile having been with us for so long, that a bull would in fact enter a china shop. In this case it was Ms. Nellie's exclusive china shop in beautiful Charleston, South Carolina, and the bull was very large.

It all happened so quickly, she wasn't quite sure what to do. She could ignore him and hope he would go away. She could show him something in an antique cream pitcher (assuming he was looking for a gift for that someone special), or she could be extremely attentive to his every whim, gush compliments about his horns, and hope he wasn't just browsing. The only thing she knew for certain was that once a bull was in your china shop, you didn't want to upset him.

The bull lingered in front of a doily-adorned glass shelf bearing a delicate display of bone china, while his tail swished closer and closer to the shelf of Ming china behind him. Ms. Nellie froze for a moment with fear. Her breath came in short, rapid puffs.

 You Can't Keep Slope Down by Faye Nisonoff Ruopp and Paula Poundstone (Heinemann: Portsmouth, NH), © 2007.

"M-m-may I h-help you?" she asked.

The bull eyed a platter that was marked 12 cm × 8 cm and the one alongside it.

"Are these two rectangular platters similar?" he asked.

"Why, yes they are. I'm glad I could help. Thank you for coming," Ms. Nellie answered eagerly.

"The long side of this platter is marked 9 cm, but the measurement of the short side is missing," said the bull, backing up and clunking his left rear hoof against the Meissen Blue Onion pattern dinner service behind him. The Meissen Blue Onion pattern dinner service, its $1,725.00 price tag, and Ms. Nellie all trembled at once.

"I can measure that for you," Ms. Nellie whispered, looking a bit like a china figurine herself. She backed slowly toward the sales counter, feeling her pockets and glancing about for her tape measure, taking her eyes off the bull for only seconds at a time. When she opened a drawer and looked into it briefly, she heard a loud thud, followed by a tinkling sound. She slammed the drawer shut.

"You're really quite light on your feet," she said nervously, hoping that saying it would make it so. There was another loud crash. The pieces of a teapot danced on the floor beside its $1,375.00 price tag. Ms. Nellie slowly lowered herself to the floor.

Please find the shorter dimension of the rectangular china platter before Ms. Nellie loses consciousness. Remember, the two rectangles are similar. The dimensions of one of them are 12 cm by 8 cm. The longer dimension of the other platter is 9 cm.

You Can't Keep Slope Down by Faye Nisonoff Ruopp and Paula Poundstone (Heinemann: Portsmouth, NH), © 2007.

Extra! Extra!

A wise person said that the character of a human being can be measured by what he does when no one is keeping track and I believe that to be true, but the measure of just about anything else requires rulers, protractors, formulas, units, and gallons of practice.

Try these:

1. Quincy says he can jump 63 centimeters. How many inches is that, if 1 cm = .3937 in.?

2. Cole measured the diameter of the circular crease around a lacrosse net and found it was 18 feet. What was the area of the crease? Leave your answer in terms of π.

3. Korbin found a lacrosse ball on the field. It was 8 inches in circumference. What was its volume, to the nearest tenth of a cubic inch?

You Can't Keep Slope Down by Faye Nisonoff Ruopp and Paula Poundstone (Heinemann: Portsmouth, NH), © 2007.

4. The height of a parallelogram is 3 feet, and its area is 72 square inches. What is the length of its base?

5. Find the volume of a cylinder if the radius of the base is 10 meters and its height is 12 meters. Leave your answer in terms of π.

6. Two right triangles are similar. The legs of one triangle are 15 feet and 20 feet, and the shorter leg of the second triangle is 6 feet. Find the length of the longer leg of the second triangle.

Teacher Notes

1. Lost Heart

For problem 1, students need to know how to convert from kilometers to miles, given the conversion factor that one mile is approximately 1.6 kilometers. The first question to answer is whether to multiply by 1.6 or divide by 1.6. It may be helpful to think about whether the answer should be greater than 5,600 or less than 5,600. In fact, the number of miles should be less than the number of kilometers, since a mile is greater than a kilometer. Therefore it makes sense to divide by 1.6. The answer is $5,600 \text{ km} \div \dfrac{1.6 \text{ km}}{\text{mi.}}$, or 3,500 miles. Another way to think about this problem is to set up a proportion that reflects the conversion factor $\dfrac{1 \text{ mi.}}{1.6 \text{ km}} = \dfrac{x \text{ mi.}}{5,600 \text{ km}}$. Multiplying both sides of the equation by 5,600 km gives the answer of $\dfrac{(1 \text{ mi.} \times 5,600 \text{ km})}{1.6 \text{ km.}}$, or 3,500 mi. Note that the units are also divided to obtain miles in the answer. Students will encounter these kinds of conversions throughout their careers, in both science and mathematics.

2. Bride and Gloom

Problem 2 requires that students recall the formula for the area of a circle ($A = \pi r^2$) and the circumference of a circle ($C = 2\pi r$). For part A, they need to find the diameter given that the area of the circle is $100\pi \text{ cm}^2$. Substituting this value for A into the area formula, we get the equation $100\pi = \pi r^2$. Dividing both sides of the equation by π, we obtain $100 = r^2$, and therefore $r = 10$. (Note that although there are two solutions to $100 = r^2$, $r = 10$ or $^-10$, we disregard $^-10$ in the context of the problem, since the length of the radius of a circle has to be a positive number.) The answer to part A is 20 cm, since we know the radius is 10 cm, and the diameter is twice 10, or 20.

For part B, since we know the radius is 10 cm, and the circumference is $2\pi r$, we can substitute 10 cm for r to get $C = 2\pi(10 \text{ cm})$, or 20π cm. (If students use 3.14 as an approximation for π, the answer is 62.8 cm.) As an extension, ask students the following question: If the radius of a circle doubles, what happens to its area? (This question has a well-known application in pricing different-size pizzas!)

3. Howdy, Neighbor!

For part A in problem 3, students need to find the length of the missing side of a trapezoid. To do this, it makes sense to construct a perpendicular line segment from A to EC, or line segment AD.

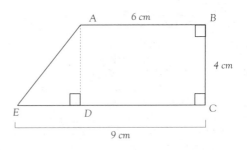

Quadrilateral *ABCD* is a rectangle, since it has four right angles. Therefore, *AD* = *BC,* and since *BC* = 4 cm, *AD* also is 4 cm. Looking at line segment EC, we know that *EC* = *ED* + *DC*, and if *EC* = 9 cm and *DC* = 6 cm (since *DC* = *AB* in rectangle *ABCD*), then *ED* = 3 cm. We now know two sides of right triangle *ADE*, and therefore to find *AE*, we can use the Pythagorean Theorem: $AE^2 = 3^2 + 4^2$, or $AE^2 = 25$, or *AE* = 5. (Note that although there are two solutions to the equation $AE^2 = 25$, 5 and ⁻5, we choose 5 since the length has to be positive in the context of the problem.)

For part B, we need to find the perimeter of the trapezoid by finding the sum of all of its sides: 6 + 4 + 9 + 5, or 24 centimeters. Since the scale is $\frac{1}{2}$ cm = 10 ft., one way to think about the actual perimeter is to find the number of half centimeters in 24 centimeters. There are 48 half centimeters in 24 centimeters, and since each of these represents 10 feet, the answer is 48 × 10, or 480 feet. Another way to think about this problem is to set up a proportion that reflects the conversion factor: $\frac{10 \text{ ft.}}{\frac{1}{2} \text{ cm}} = \frac{x \text{ ft.}}{24 \text{ cm}}$.

Multiplying both sides of the equation by 24 cm gives the answer of $\frac{24 \text{ cm } (10 \text{ ft.})}{\frac{1}{2} \text{ cm}}$, or 480 ft.

The simplest way to think about part C in problem 3 is to realize that the house lot is in the shape of a trapezoid. Since the side of length 6 centimeters and the side of length 9 centimeters are both perpendicular to the side of length 4 centimeters, these two sides must be parallel; therefore, the figure is a trapezoid. Students need to know the formula for the area of a trapezoid: $\frac{1}{2}h(b_1 + b_2)$, or one-half the height times the sum of the bases. Since the bases are the parallel sides, and the height is the side of length 4 centimeters because it is perpendicular to the base, the area is $\frac{1}{2}$ (4 cm)(6 cm + 9 cm), or 30 square centimeters.

An interesting way to think about this area formula is to consider a dissection of the trapezoid—that is, cutting the trapezoid to form another polygon so that area is preserved. Any trapezoid can be dissected into a parallelogram: find the midpoints of the two nonparallel sides, connect them with a line segment, and cut along the line segment. Now rotate the upper half clockwise so that the two congruent sides coincide. A parallelogram is formed, with one set of parallel sides equal to the sum of the bases of the original trapezoid. The height of the parallelogram is half the height of the original trapezoid. Therefore to find the area of the parallelogram (base times height), we are multiplying the sum of the original trapezoid's bases and half of the original trapezoid's height.

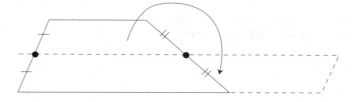

As an extension, ask students if they can dissect any trapezoid to form a triangle.

4. Leonardo the Lifetime Learner and the Decimals of Doom

For problem 4 students need to determine the surface area of a cylinder. If they do not remember the formula, ask them to think about taking a sheet of paper and folding it to form the lateral surface of a cylinder. In fact, the lateral area is the area of a rectangle, where one of the dimensions is the same as the height of the cylinder, and the other dimension is the circumference of the circle that forms its base.

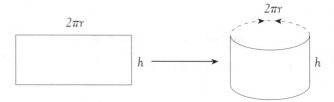

Therefore the total surface area is the sum of the lateral area and the areas of the two circular bases: $2\pi rh + 2\pi r^2$. The information given in the problem tells us the height, but we need to do some additional work to find the radius. Since we know the volume is 325π cubic feet, and the formula for the volume of a cylinder is $V = \pi r^2 h$ (the area of the base times the height), we have $325\pi = \pi r^2 h$. Since $h = 13$, we get $325\pi = \pi r^2(13)$. Dividing both sides by π and then by 13, we get $r^2 = 25$, or $r = 5$ (selecting the positive value only since the radius has to be a positive number). Now we are ready to find the surface area, or $2\pi rh + 2\pi r^2$, by substituting $h = 13$ and $r = 5$, to get $2\pi(5)(13) + 2\pi(5)^2$, or $130\pi + 50\pi$, or 180π square feet. (If students use 3.14 as an approximation for π, the answer is 565.2 square feet). As an extension, ask students to find the surface area of a sphere with the same volume as this cylinder.

5. Up with Pins

For problem 5, students need to know the formula for the volume of a sphere: $V = \frac{4}{3}\pi r^3$. Unfortunately, this formula is not as intuitive as other volume formulas (e.g., the volume of a prism or a cylinder) that can be generalized as the area of the base times the height. However, students may find it helpful to visualize the following: the volume of a hemisphere is halfway between the volume of a cone and the volume of a cylinder with the same radius and height equal to the radius.

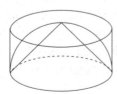

The volume of the cylinder is $\pi r^2 \times r$ or πr^3, and the volume of the cone is $\frac{1}{3}\pi r^2 \times r$ or $\frac{1}{3}\pi r^3$. The volume of the hemisphere is halfway between these, or $\frac{2}{3}\pi r^3$. Doubling the hemisphere's volume, $2(\frac{2}{3}\pi r^3)$, yields the volume of a sphere, which is equal to $\frac{4}{3}\pi r^3$. To find the volume of the sphere in problem 5, substitute 3 inches for the radius: $V = \frac{4}{3}\pi(3)^3$, or 36π cubic inches.

As an extension, ask students the following question: If you have an ice-cream cone and a sphere of ice cream on top, both with diameter 8 cm, and you push the ice cream into the cone, what is the smallest height for the cone that will make the ice cream fit?

6. Exactly Like a Bull in a China Shop

For problem 6, students need to know that similar figures have corresponding sides that are in the same ratio. To find the shorter dimension of the other rectangle, they can set up a proportion for the corresponding dimensions: $\frac{8 \text{ cm}}{12 \text{ cm}} = \frac{x \text{ cm}}{9 \text{ cm}}$. Multiplying both sides of the equation by 9 centimeters, the equation becomes $\frac{8 \text{ cm}(9 \text{ cm})}{12 \text{ cm}} = x \text{ cm}$, or $x = 6$ cm. Students may set up other proportions that are also correct, such as

$$\frac{x \text{ cm}}{8 \text{ cm}} = \frac{9 \text{ cm}}{12 \text{ cm}}$$

Extra! Extra!

1. 24.8031 inches
2. 81π square feet
3. 8.6 cubic inches
4. 2 inches
5. $1{,}200\pi$ cubic meters
6. 8 feet

You Can't Keep Slope Down by Faye Nisonoff Ruopp and Paula Poundstone (Heinemann: Portsmouth, NH), © 2007.

Data Analysis, Statistics & Probability

The problems that follow are in the Data Analysis, Statistics, and Probability strand. The mathematics in these problems focuses on developing students' skills in comparing data sets as they interpret and use measures of central tendency. Students in grades 8 and 9 construct and analyze different representations of data such as Venn diagrams, scatter plots, stem-and-leaf plots, box-and-whisker plots, and histograms. This strand also includes approximating lines of best fit as well as the probability of compound events.

The topics covered in these problems were chosen from state and national standards:

- Create graphical representations of data, such as circle graphs, Venn diagrams, scatter plots, stem-and-leaf plots, box-and-whisker plots, histograms, tables, and charts

- Interpret appropriate measures of central tendency (mean, median, and mode) and range to compare different sets of data

- Approximate lines of best fit

- Predict the probability of outcomes of simple compound events such as multiple coin tosses

Broadway's Hottest Star Overheats

On the third consecutive day that New York City's temperature reached triple digits, Broadway's brightest and most beloved star, Rebecca Encore Porter, cracked. After enchanting audiences for thirty years in every theatre on the Great White Way, she was pushed over the edge by this heat wave. She was throwing in her makeup sponge and kicking out the footlights of the big-city stage for the last time. She was bowing out. The final curtain was coming down.

Her manager, Buddy Fella, tried to talk her out of it, but as he stood looking at the greatest actress the world had ever known, her hair inflated with humidity, her face drooping, and her delicate silk blouse adhered to her body with sweat, he realized he wasn't making much headway.

"Darling! How can you leave New York City? What could you be thinking?"

"Sweat," she answered dazedly.

"How can you turn your back on your career?" Buddy pleaded.

"I can't. My shirt's stuck to my chair," she answered, not moving a muscle.

"Rebecca Encore Porter, you are Broadway; Broadway is you! You've been Annie in *Annie*. You've been Beauty in *Beauty and the Beast*. You practically produced *The Producers*. You were a lot in *Spam-a-Lot*. You coughed up a fur ball in *Cats*.

You Can't Keep Slope Down by Faye Nisonoff Ruopp and Paula Poundstone (Heinemann: Portsmouth, NH), © 2007.

"You are the lights of New York City!" Buddy roared with enthusiasm.

"I'll be the flashlight of San Diego," Rebecca said, looking like a fallen shower curtain.

"Here's a table of the average maximum monthly temperatures in New York City. It's a little uncomfortable now, I know, but it'll pass," Buddy Fella said, and he held the paper with the table on it in front of her face. "Think of the Empire State Building. Think of Central Park. Think about the museums, the nightlife, and the crowds of people living and working in the richest tapestry of human beings under the sun."

Rebecca's thighs slid forward on a puddle of her sweat that had collected on the chair, like a melting pat of butter.

"Send me a postcard," she said weakly from the floor.

"Maybe if she looked at the data in a different way," thought Buddy Fella.

Help Buddy Fella save the best thing to hit New York City since pizza.

MONTH	AVERAGE MAXIMUM TEMP IN FAHRENHEIT
January	39
February	40
March	48
April	61
May	71
June	81
July	85
August	83
September	77
October	67
November	54
December	41

A. Create a stem-and-leaf plot of the temperatures.

B. Create a histogram of the temperatures.

You Can't Keep Slope Down by Faye Nisonoff Ruopp and Paula Poundstone (Heinemann: Portsmouth, NH), © 2007.

C. Create a box-and-whisker plot of the temperatures.

D. Create a line graph of the temperatures.

E. Which graph seems most useful for finding the median average maximum temperature for the year? What is the median?

F. Which graph seems most useful for finding the range in temperatures?

G. Which graph gives the most information about the trend in temperatures over the year?

Pedals from Heaven

It was a good thing that Marcus went over his supply checklist carefully the day before his cross-country bicycle trip for Habitat for Humanity because he noticed a few things he would have regretted not having.

"Let's see," he mumbled, "gotta get an abrasive scrubber for stubborn cooked-on foods on pots, gotta get bungee chords in assorted sizes, energy bars, oh, and a bicycle. Silly me."

He then pocketed his list and headed out to secure the missing necessaries.

With his head spinning after spending an hour torn between the array of choices at Al's Abrasive Scrubbers, he proceeded to Pedals from Heaven, the Chain Gang, Spokes Folks, Raise My Seat, the Pump Palace, the Bicycle Store, and the House of B, a place whose entire inventory consisted of things that began with the letter B that was said to have a quality selection of bikes tucked between the bacon and the belts. He informed the salesperson in every store he went into that he would be riding 70 miles a day for 50 days, so he was looking for a reasonably priced bicycle without a lot of frills. He needed to save his money for chafing creams and the medical care he was likely to require after the trip. That didn't stop a persuasive young lad working for commissions at the Squeaky Wheel from showing him the high-end TR460 model that came with an escalator for easy mounting.

Nor did it put off the salesman at the Pump Palace, who tried desperately to interest him in a bike fully loaded with video and editing capability so that the cycling enthusiast could send loved ones daily updates of his journey with the unflattering sounds of his grunting and wheezing tastefully edited out.

Marcus wasn't sure that the trip could be any more grueling than spending hours repeatedly telling a guy recently honored at the Calf and Thigh Club that he didn't need gold pedals and that even just $200 extra was more than he wanted to pay for a really good bell.

He was seriously considering just fixing up his old tricycle when he staggered out of Raise My Seat, the last bicycle store from which he collected price data, where a salesman employed his every sales tactic to convince Marcus that he wouldn't make it back alive without purchasing the Land Eater 5,000 12-speed one-bedroom bicycle featuring a computerized navigation system that could tell him how far he was from Ryan Seacrest's birthplace at all times.

"Girls love it," the salesman quickly added when Marcus stared lifelessly instead of going for his wallet.

"I'll come back," said Marcus, backing slowly away.

He came up with this set of retail prices from the various bike stores:

$450, $300, $275, $325, $600, $725, $550

A. Find the mean price for this set of stores.

B. Find the median price for this set of stores.

You Can't Keep Slope Down by Faye Nisonoff Ruopp and Paula Poundstone (Heinemann: Portsmouth, NH), © 2007.

Marcus then found a store that carried a bicycle that had just been developed that was supposed to be the best in the world. It sold for $2,000. It had cable TV.

C. What is the new mean price? How much does it differ from the old mean?

D. What is the new median price? How much does it differ from the old median?

E. If you were shopping for a new bike, would it be more helpful to know the mean or median price?

F. Explain the effect of an outlier on the mean and the median.

You Can't Keep Slope Down by Faye Nisonoff Ruopp and Paula Poundstone (Heinemann: Portsmouth, NH), © 2007.

The Incalculable Joy of Accounting

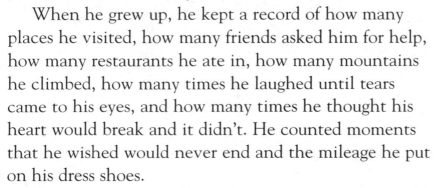

Albert was a very successful accountant. He had always loved to keep a tally. When he was a young boy, he kept track of how many times he rode his bike around the block by scratching a stick in the wet dirt at the edge of the woods behind his house. He kept a record of how many different kinds of birds he saw and of how many books he read.

When he grew up, he kept a record of how many places he visited, how many friends asked him for help, how many restaurants he ate in, how many mountains he climbed, how many times he laughed until tears came to his eyes, and how many times he thought his heart would break and it didn't. He counted moments that he wished would never end and the mileage he put on his dress shoes.

He loved to count. He insisted that his wife, Mary, count off every morning. "Albert," she'd complain, "why do I need to count off? There's only one of me."

"That's right," he'd say with a smile and wait for her to bristle with annoyance before she'd reluctantly shout, "One!"

"Why do you do all of that counting?" Mary once asked him.

"Because, when you keep track of money for a living, there's always the possibility that you'll forget what makes a man rich, and when my one wonderful wife counts off, I am reminded that I have so much," he said.

You Can't Keep Slope Down by Faye Nisonoff Ruopp and Paula Poundstone (Heinemann: Portsmouth, NH), © 2007.

She began to cry and Albert quickly jotted down how many tears ran softly down her cheeks.

Tax season, the month or two before tax day, April 15, the day Americans pay a percentage of their income to the government, was always stressful and busy for Albert, as it was his job to figure out how much money his clients owed the government. Of course, after he calculated his clients' debt, he calculated his own. Early in the morning one April 14, Mary found him still at his desk from the night before, surrounded by papers and pizza, exhausted, irritable, dejected, and mumbling something about quitting accounting, not caring about gross income or balance and never tallying again.

His wife had never seen him this far gone. Looking for a way to bring him back to his senses, she spotted a table Albert had made for keeping track of the number of clients he had had over the last 10 years. She placed it on the desk in front of him.

"Albert, you love being an accountant. You're just tired. Look at this table. Look at how many people you've helped. Come on, honey, let's graph the data. You'll feel better," she said gently. He smiled slightly, but when he tried to nod his head, he fell face first into a slice of cold pizza.

He's still awake, though. How about if you analyze the data and show it to him?

YEAR	1997	1998	1999	2000	2001	2002	2003	2004	2005	2006
NUMBER OF CLIENTS	15	25	45	40	55	55	60	70	85	95

A. Graph the data.

You Can't Keep Slope Down by Faye Nisonoff Ruopp and Paula Poundstone (Heinemann: Portsmouth, NH), © 2007.

B. Do the data appear to be approximately linear?

C. Are there any outliers, or points that do not seem to fit the general trend of the data? If so, what are they?

D. Draw a line that fits the data as well as possible and that goes through the point (mean number of years, mean number of clients), and find its equation.

What Are the Odds of Slope Being Tossed on His Head?

For the first ten laps around the one-room schoolhouse that Slope chased his classmate known as Luckless Lloyd, who was chasing Sarah Sue Simmons with a stick with possum guts on it, Lloyd remained a maddening inch from Slope's grasp. Worried that his legs would give out altogether, Slope finally just panted out, "Lloyd, what are you doing?"

"I'm Luckless Lloyd and I'm tryin' to get me a girl," Luckless Lloyd shouted back, kicking up a bigger cloud of dust as he put on speed. No doubt motivated by the oncoming stick bearing possum guts, and despite the wind resistance caused by her bonnet that billowed behind her head while anchored around her throat, Sarah Sue Simmons maintained a commanding lead.

"I don't think you are luckless, Lloyd," shouted Slope.

"Of course I am. I just flunked another mathematics test, and my slate done broke again today," Luckless Lloyd yelled back.

"Your slate broke because you hit me with it, just like yesterday, and did you study for the arithmetic test?" puffed Slope, still straining to keep up with the flying feet in front of him.

"Say what?" yelled Luckless Lloyd, baffled by the very question.

"If you didn't study and you flunked a test, that's not bad luck, that's what's probable," Slope said.

You Can't Keep Slope Down by Faye Nisonoff Ruopp and Paula Poundstone (Heinemann: Portsmouth, NH), © 2007.

"What?" demanded Luckless Lloyd, coming to a stop, much to the relief of both Sarah Sue Simmons, who sprinted out of sight, and Slope, who, pleased to have finally gotten through to Luckless Lloyd, slowly repeated, "If you didn't study and you flunked a test, that's not bad luck, that's what's probable."

Luckless Lloyd thought for a second, taking this in, looked the smiling Slope in the eye, and calmly stated, "I am going to pluck you like a chicken," before pouncing on Slope and pinning him to the ground.

"Look Lloyd, there's a greater likelihood of some things happening than others, and this can sometimes be determined mathematically; it is called probability," Slope persisted, struggling beneath Luckless Lloyd.

Lloyd's fist was now drawn back, perilously aimed at Slope's face, and there was a great probability that it would smash into his face within seconds, but Slope quickly continued, "If you think in terms of probability, you'll have a better chance of forming a nice relationship with a girl."

Luckless Lloyd's fist lowered, so Slope ventured on. "There aren't many people who like to be chased with a stick, and if it's a girl you're looking for, there are even fewer. Now, you put possum guts on the end of your stick and you're gonna find that that reduces dramatically the group of girls that seek out a fella who will chase 'em with it. The girls who will seek out a fella who will chase them with a stick with possum guts on it, with love in their hearts, are rare indeed."

"Explain more to me about this here probability," said Lloyd, intrigued.

"Well, for example, if you toss a coin and a die, there's a certain probability that the coin will land on heads and the die will show a 4."

"What is it?" interrupted Luckless Lloyd.

"I don't know," Slope stammered. "I'm just using an example. I'd have to figure it out."

"You're makin' this up and now my beloved has run off and left me!" howled Luckless Lloyd.

Quick, tell Slope what the probability is that the coin will land on heads and the die will show a 4 when a coin and a die are tossed, before a coin, a die, and Slope are tossed.

Extra! Extra!

Statistics show that four out of five students who do extra practice problems in data analysis, statistics, and probability get great pleasure from it and the fifth gets very good at data analysis, statistics, and probability.

1. **Mrs. Ross teaches piano. The following numbers are the ages of her students:**

13   8   18   6   11   9   12   7   14   23   7   11
  8   13   5   6   20   11   14   8   13   32   21   9

A. Create a stem-and-leaf plot of the ages.

B. Create a histogram of the ages.

C. Create a box-and-whisker plot of the ages.

D. Find the mean age, to the nearest hundredth.

E. Find the median age.

2. At Newton North High School, a total of 100 students tried out for the soccer team, a total of 120 students tried out for the lacrosse team, and 30 students tried out for both. Draw a Venn Diagram that represents this situation.

3. A. Draw a scatter plot of the following data:

TIMES AT BAT	6	3	5	2	6	7	2	4	3	7
NUMBER OF HITS	5	1	3	1	3	5	2	2	3	4

B. Draw a line of best fit for the scatter plot in part A.

C. What would you predict for the number of hits for 9 times at bat?

4. A spinner is divided into five equal sections labeled 1 through 5. Find the probability of getting a 3 on the spinner and heads on a coin if you spin the spinner and toss the coin at the same time.

You Can't Keep Slope Down by Faye Nisonoff Ruopp and Paula Poundstone (Heinemann: Portsmouth, NH), © 2007.

Teacher Notes

1. Broadway's Hottest Star Overheats

For part A of problem 1, students are given a table of data that includes twelve months of different average maximum temperatures for New York City. In a stem-and-leaf plot, the stems are the digits that appear in the left-hand column, and each digit on the right is a leaf. For the numbers in this table, the stems would be the tens digits, and the leaves would be the ones digits. The stem-and-leaf plot would be:

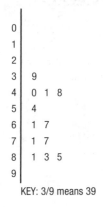

```
0
1
2
3 | 9
4 | 0 1 8
5 | 4
6 | 1 7
7 | 1 7
8 | 1 3 5
9
```
KEY: 3/9 means 39

For part B, students are asked to make a histogram, a graph that displays the frequency of data. The first step in creating a histogram is to create equal intervals for the horizontal axis, which will be the width of the bars. Intervals of 5 degrees seem reasonable. The height of a bar will represent the number of data values (here, the number of months) in that interval, or the frequency. A separate table can be created to do this.

AVG. MAX. TEMP.	NUMBER OF OCCURENCES
35–39	1
40–44	2
45–49	1
50–54	1
55–59	0
60–64	1
65–69	1
70–74	1
75–79	1
80–84	2
85–90	1

For example, in the interval from 40 to 45, there are two values in the table, 40 and 41. Therefore the height for the bar will be 2. A possible histogram for these data is the following:

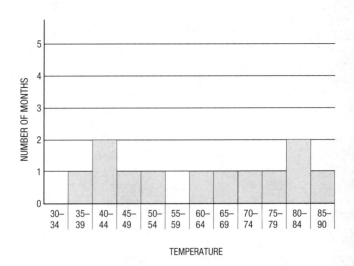

You Can't Keep Slope Down by Faye Nisonoff Ruopp and Paula Poundstone (Heinemann: Portsmouth, NH), © 2007.

For part C, students need to construct a box-and-whisker plot of the temperatures. A box-and-whisker plot separates the data into four groups: two whiskers and a box with two parts. The data points that divide the sections are quartiles, and the second quartile is the median. The first step in creating a box-and-whisker plot is to find the minimum and maximum data points, which we can determine from the table. The minimum temperature is 39 and the maximum temperature is 85. These two points will be the first and last points, respectively, in the plot at the end of each whisker. The next step is to find the median temperature value, the value in the middle when the temperatures are placed in order. The median can be found easily from the stem-and-leaf plot created in part A by counting from each end to the middle values, or 61 and 67. Note that since there are an even number of values, 12, there is no middle value; to find the median, we take the average of the two middle values. The average of 61 and 67 is 64, the median. In this case the median is not a point in the data set. Now we need to find the first and third quartiles. Looking at the data points less than 64 (these are 61, 54, 48, 41, 40, and 39), the first quartile is the median of these six values, or the average of 48 and 41, or 44.5. The third quartile is the median of the data points greater than 64 (these are 67, 71, 77, 81, 83, and 85), found by taking the average of 77 and 81, or 79. We can now draw the box-and-whisker plots with the minimum, first quartile, second quartile (median), third quartile, and maximum values:

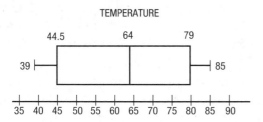

For part D, students need to construct a line graph of the average maximum monthly temperatures. Line graphs are helpful in showing changes in data over time. Following is a line graph for this data:

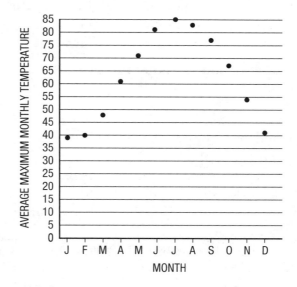

For part E, students need to determine the graph most useful for finding the median. Since the median is the second quartile in a box-and-whisker plot and is one of the five points needed to construct the plot, it is easiest to observe where the median lies in a box-and-whisker plot. The median for this set of data is 64.

The graph most useful for finding the range for part F would again be the box-and-whisker plot since the endpoints of the plot are the minimum and maximum points, the points that determine the range.

For part G, students need to consider which graph shows change in temperature over time. The line graph gives the most information about trends since the horizontal axis displays the months in order, unlike the stem-and-leaf plot, the histogram, and the box-and-whisker plot.

You Can't Keep Slope Down by Faye Nisonoff Ruopp and Paula Poundstone (Heinemann: Portsmouth, NH), © 2007.

2. Pedals from Heaven

Students need to find the mean price of bicycles for part A in problem 2. To find the mean, they need to add up all the prices and divide by the number of prices. The sum 450 + 300 + 275 + 325 + 600 + 725 + 550 is 3,225. There are seven values, and therefore the mean is $\frac{3,225}{7}$, or $460.71.

For part B, students need to put the prices in order and find the middle price. In order the prices are 275, 300, 325, 450, 550, 600, 725. The median is the fourth value, or $450. As an extension, ask students to add one additional price to the seven prices given so that mean remains the same.

For part C, the additional value of $2,000 is added to the list. The new total is 3,225 + 2,000, or 5,225. The mean is $\frac{5,225}{8}$, or $653.13. The difference between $653.13 and the mean calculated in part B is $653.13 − $460.71, or $192.42.

Students need to calculate the new median price for part D. Since one additional value ($2,000) has been added to the bike prices, there are now eight values. The median is the average of the middle two values (the list is now 275, 300, 325, 450, 550, 600, 725, 2000), or $\frac{450 + 550}{2}$, or $500. The difference between $500 and the median calculated in part B is $500 – $450, or $50.

For part E, students need to realize that the added eighth value, $2,000, is an outlier in the data set of bike prices, since it is very different from the others. Therefore when thinking about the meaning of *average* price, it is more helpful to know the median price since it is less affected by the outlier. The answer to part F is that in general, an outlier has less of an effect on the median than on the mean since it will not distort the "typical" price.

3. The Incalculable Joy of Accounting

For part A in problem 3, students need to graph the data representing the year and the number of clients in that year. The graph is

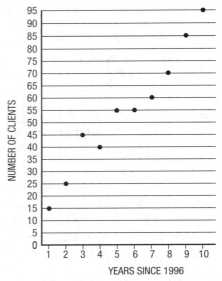

For part B, students need to determine whether the data represent an approximate linear pattern. The graph displays points that cluster to form a line, and therefore the data appear to be approximately linear.

In part C, students need to determine if there are any outliers in the data. An outlier is a data point that seems very different from other points in the data set. Outliers are generally extreme values much greater or much less than the other values in the set. Since they can distort means, they are generally discarded. Although there is one point that is farther away from the linear trend in this data than others (the number of clients in 1999), this would probably not be considered an outlier since it would not skew the mean.

For part D, students need to compute the mean number of years and the mean number of clients. The mean year is halfway between 2001 and 2002, or 5.5 on the graph. The mean number of clients is the total number of clients for these ten years (15 + 25 + 45 + 40 + 55 + 55 + 60 + 70 + 85 + 95, or 545) divided by the number of years, or $\frac{545}{10}$, or 54.5. Therefore the line of best fit should go through the point (5.5, 54.5) with approximately as many points on either side of it. A reasonable line of best fit is the following:

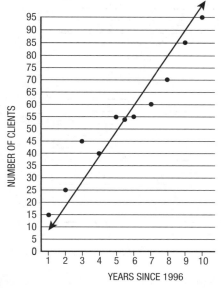

As an extension, some students may be interested in entering this data into a graphing calculator. The graphing calculator determines the line of best fit through a method of least squares, which minimizes the distance from the data points to the line. Ask students how close this line is to the line they created using the means of the data.

4. What Are the Odds of Slope Being Tossed on His Head?

Students should make either a table or a tree diagram to answer problem 4. A table of all possible outcomes of tossing a coin and a die is the following:

	1	2	3	4	5	6
H	H, 1	H, 2	H, 3	H, 4	H, 5	H, 6
T	T, 1	T, 2	T, 3	T, 4	T, 5	T, 6

There are twelve possible outcomes, and only one of them is (H, 4). Therefore the probability is $\frac{1}{12}$.

A tree diagram of all possible outcomes is the following:

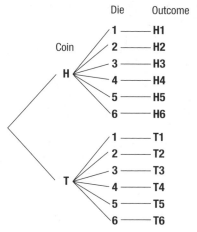

Again, there is one outcome out of twelve of tossing a heads and a 4.

As an extension, ask students to find the probability of tossing 4 twice if the coin and a die are tossed twice.

Extra! Extra!

1. A.

```
0 | 5 6 6 7 7 8 8 8 9 9
1 | 1 1 1 2 3 3 3 4 4 8
2 | 0 1 3
3 | 2
```

KEY: 0/5 means 5

B.

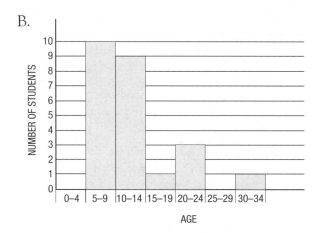

You Can't Keep Slope Down by Faye Nisonoff Ruopp and Paula Poundstone (Heinemann: Portsmouth, NH), © 2007.

C.

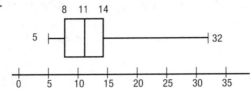

D. 12.46

E. 11

2.

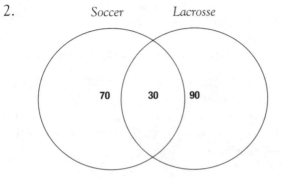

3. A.

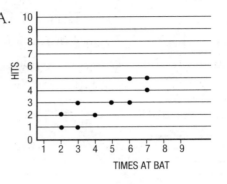

B.

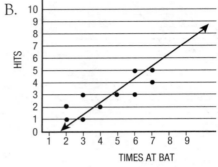

C. approximately 7

4. $\dfrac{1}{10}$